AUSTRALIA

GOOD STORIES REVEAL as much, or more, about a locale as any map or guidebook. Whereabouts Press is dedicated to publishing books that will enlighten a traveler to the soul of a place. By bringing a country's stories to the English-speaking reader, we hope to convey its culture through literature. Books from Whereabouts Press are essential companions for the curious traveler, and for the person who appreciates how fine writing enhances one's experiences in the world.

"Coming newly into Spanish, I lacked two essentials —a childhood in the language, which I could never acquire, and a sense of its literature, which I could."

—Alastair Reid, *Whereabouts:
Notes on Being a Foreigner*

OTHER TRAVELER'S LITERARY COMPANIONS

Costa Rica edited by Barbara Ras
with a foreword by Oscar Arias

Prague edited by Paul Wilson

Vietnam edited by John Balaban
and Nguyen Qui Duc

Israel edited by Michael Gluzman and Naomi Seidman
with a foreword by Robert Alter

Greece edited by Artemis Leontis

Gay Travels (available May 1998) and *Lesbian Travels*
(available September 1998) edited by Lucy Jane Bledsoe

AUSTRALIA

A TRAVELER'S LITERARY COMPANION

EDITED BY

ROBERT ROSS

WHEREABOUTS PRESS
SAN FRANCISCO

Published in the United States by
Whereabouts Press
2219 Clement Street, Suite 18
San Francisco, California 94121
www.whereaboutspress.com

Distributed to the trade by
Consortium Book Sales & Distribution

Map of Australia by Bill Nelson

Manufactured in the United States of America

Library of Congress Cataloging-in-Publication Data

Australia / edited by Robert L. Ross.
   p.   cm. (a traveler's literary companion)
 ISBN 1-883513-05-7 (alk. paper)
  1. Australia—Social life and customs—Fiction.   2. Short
stories, Australian.   I. Ross, Robert.   II. Series.
PR9617.32.A9   1998
821'.01083294—dc21
                                    97–47562
                                       CIP

5   4   3   2

Contents

Preface

"SYDNEY OR THE BUSH! All or nothing!" This saying from nineteenth-century Australia represents life in the city as "all," its opposite as "nothing." Such an odd sentiment still sums up a key conflict in Australia. Today there are 18 million or so people on a land mass about the size of the United States, yet nearly 70 percent of them live in the capital cities, each one set along the coast: Sydney, Brisbane, Melbourne, Adelaide, Hobart, and Perth. Beyond this fringe of settlement lies The Bush. Although the term simply describes unsettled regions—whether forest, mountains, desert, or rolling hills, it carried larger implications during the colonial period, and continues to do so in Australia. Arguments still rage over whether or not The Bush formed national character and symbolizes the true Australia, free of the cities, which Australian poet A.D. Hope called "five teeming sores" that infect the land. Many city-dwelling Australians would rather forget what is sometimes called the outback or the back of the beyond and all the mystery it supposedly holds. They are more likely to travel to Europe or the United States.

Travelers to Australia immediately discover for themselves the terrifying power of the vast emptiness once they leave sophisticated cities like Sydney or Melbourne, where they usually start out. If they are literary travelers as well, they need not be "Lost in The Bush" to revive a colonial fear that evolved into myth. For the writers have charted a way, starting with the continent's original inhabitants who dwelled on the land for 40 thousand or so years in happy isolation until 1788, when the first Europeans settled. In this book's opening selections, two Aboriginal writers draw from their rich tradition to present a creation myth, then to ask that all people recognize the land's mystique. Australia's first literature was oral, and anthropologists in recent years have collected these stories. Many of them explain natural phenomena, which "Man-and-Kangaroo Rock" in this collection illustrates.

With settlement came a written literature. It first took the form of reports sent to England on practical matters, on the unfamiliar flora and fauna, and on the natives. Before long, though, poets and storytellers tried their hand at relating what the land and life on it were like. So began the bush tradition in Australian writing, which dominated well into the twentieth century even as the cities grew. While the tradition and its main actor, the swaggering, self-reliant bushman, have faded, reincarnations do occur now and then. Such was the case with Crocodile Dundee, charming millions abroad while embarrassing many Australians, who felt that the character drew an inaccurate picture of their country in the late twentieth century.

One of the liveliest practitioners in the bush tradition was Henry Lawson. In "His Country—After All," Lawson shows the uncertainty with which the settler Australians and their descendants sometimes view the land. While they may not see it as sacred or mythical or beautiful or worth all that much, they will in the end, Lawson suggests, remain true to their roots.

Another subject that has long intrigued Australian writers stems from the country's settlement by convicts, who have been called "the reluctant pioneers." The selection here from Eleanor Dark's *The Timeless Land* lets modern travelers imagine how that first tour group, the convicts and their keepers, reacted on arrival at a destination they had not chosen. In fact, today's tourists will most likely make their way to The Rocks, the name given to the area along Sydney Harbor where the First Fleet finally landed in January 1788, and where the sermon recorded in "The First Gathering" was delivered. No sermons now, though, along The Rocks, which has reinvented itself into a place of smart clubs and cafés, theaters, trendy shops, hotels and condominiums.

Once the Transportation System—as the practice of dumping British convicts in Australia was called—ended in the 1830s, free settlers, speculators, and adventurers arrived. While some did indeed learn to love the land and its strangeness, others came to see the vast continent as inhospitable, cruel, and beguiling, a place where they endured isolation, dust, flies, fire, drought, floods, and a thousand other calamities. These contrasting views have been captured by Australia's writers, sometimes in tragic tones, at other times through comedy. Even if the literary travelers do not get far into The Bush or stay there long enough for it to work its spell, they may still experience it through the stories this book offers. They can attend a mythical dingo picnic; watch a kangaroo hunt firsthand; discover the horrors of a land Barbara Baynton called the "wind-blown, shimmering, shifting, awful waste"; join the inept Rudd family to hunt bears; cheer at a makeshift horse race; visit a bush household kept by the O'Dowds; share one woman's joy in the land; or take a meaningful walk through the Northern Tropics.

Australia has always been a place of distances, of passages, of movement from one region to another. Tim Winton takes the reader on a modern passage, a three-thousand-mile flight from Perth to its neighboring city of Melbourne. While Thea Astley's train rider covers little ground, she revels in the events that occur during her passage through the spectacular scenery of the Northern Queensland rainforest, then rejoices in the miracle she senses on her arrival. Katharine Susannah Prichard revisits a once-important passage, Western Australia's old "track" that provided access to the interior and its potential riches.

Living on a continent surrounded by magnificent stretches of white sand, Australians have developed a true beach culture. This passion for the land's seductive edge, far from the barren waste of the interior, often makes its way into the literature. Set in the famous beach settlement called Surfers Paradise, Helen Garner's story examines the conflicts that arise when a prodigal daughter joins her family for a vacation at the seashore—a time-honored Australian tradition. And Robert Drewe's character, even while celebrating the miraculous quality of Sydney's popular Bondi Beach, discovers an ugly, poisonous side in the waters and in the urban sprawl beyond the sands.

If, like so many before them, the new visitors to Australia leave The Bush behind and cross the dramatic border into The City, they will find an infinite variety there. Each of Australia's metropolitan areas has its own ambience and charm, whether large and cosmopolitan like Sydney and Melbourne, or smaller and more provincial like Hobart, Brisbane, and Adelaide, or exotic and remote like Perth. Following World War II and Australia's entry into the larger world, young city-bred writers shunned the fading bush tradition and wrote about The City—"Their Place—After All," to recast Lawson's title.

The urban traveler is immediately transported to Sydney's colorful King's Cross by Mandy Sayer, as she depicts a comic encounter between visiting American sailors and a local boy. Still in Sydney, Michael Wilding pokes a little fun at the city's literary culture. In selections that are more memoir than narrative, C. J. Koch describes his hometown of Hobart on the island of Tasmania, a place haunted by its convict past; and David Malouf brings to life one steamy tropical afternoon in Brisbane where he grew up.

After 1945 thousands of European refugees came to Australia and changed its Anglo-Celtic character forever; Judah Waten tells of one such family who settled in Melbourne. Each of the cities, their centers still vital, are surrounded by suburbs, and Murray Bail gives an improbable version of the afternoon barbecue, a true Australian-suburban tradition. Archie Weller's account of the Aboriginal deprived of his heritage and adrift in Perth typifies much of the recent writing by Aboriginals, who see literature as a way to reveal and to protest their precarious position within a society controlled by a majority of European descent.

In an imaginative departure from the other stories, Peter Carey in "American Dreams" creates a fantasy touching on many of the subjects that dominate current Australian thinking and writing: national identity in a post-colonial nation; American influence—especially in popular culture; and the selling of Australia as a tourist destination specializing in nostalgia.

Whether the travelers with this volume in hand wanted it or not, they have been subjected in this preface to a short history of Australian literature, and at the same time a historical account of Australia, along with a geography lesson. These topics are, after all, intertwined. Still, wouldn't it be more reliable to consult a history book, not fiction, for information on the country's original inhabitants, its settlers, and their efforts and failures at expansion? Wouldn't a geography book or even some pamphlets from a tourist bureau better describe a particular city or the mysteries of The Bush?

So what do reading travelers discover in literature that they wouldn't find in histories, reference books, and brochures? Perhaps Thea Astley best answered the question: "Literary truth is derived from the parish, and if it is truth it will be universal." While this little collection draws deeply from the Australian "parish" and makes known its parts, each story offers infinitely more—the revelation of essential truths about the human condition, whatever the parish.

Robert Ross

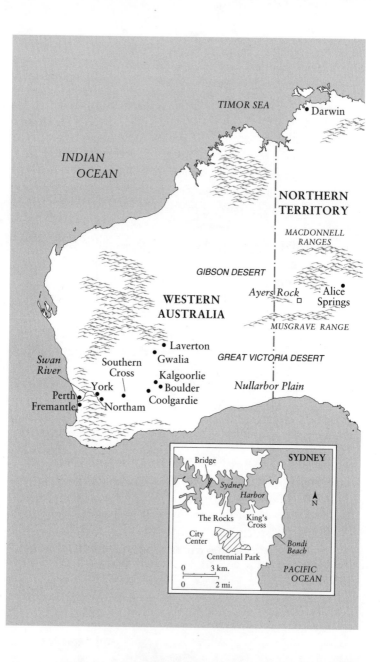

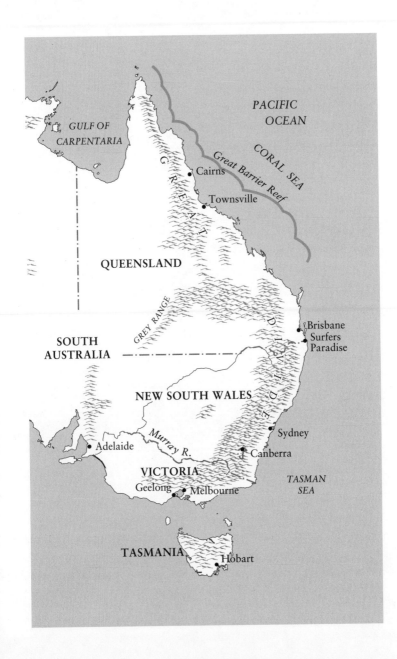

The Rainbow Serpent

Oodgeroo Noonuccal
Kabul Oodgeroo Noonuccal

WELL, GIDDAY, GIDDAY, all you earth fullas. Come, sit down, my country now. I see you come into sacred place of my tribe to get the strength of the Earth Mother That Earth Mother . . . We are different you and me. We say the earth is our mother—we cannot own her, she own us.

This rock and all these rocks are alive with her spirit. They protect us, all of us. They are her, what you fullas say now, temple. Since the Alcheringa, that thing you fulla call Dreamtime, this place has given man shelter from the heat, a place to paint, to dance the sacred dance and talk to his spirit. How does one repay such gifts? By protecting the land. This land is the home of the Dreamtime. The spirits came and painted themselves on these walls so that man could meet here, grow strong again, and take this strength back into the world.

This my totem, Kabul. You know her as the Carpet Snake. She my tribe's symbol of the Rainbow Serpent, the giver and taker of life. Sometimes she is called Borlung, sometimes Ngalyod. She has many names, that wise one. When the spirits of men have been made strong again by

Kabul, she'll come back to this earth. But we are not strong now. We are too tired from fighting time, machines, and each other.

But she send her spirit ones with message sticks to help us take time. To remember. To care for special things. First there is Dooruk, the emu, with the dust of the red Earth Mother still on his feet. He come to remind us to protect the land, to always put back as much as we take. Then there is Kopoo, the big red kangaroo, the very color of the land. He come to remind us to always take time for ourselves. And Mungoongarlie, the goanna, last of all because his legs are short. He bring the news that we, his children, are forgetting to give time to each other. But the animals of the Earth Mother come to say more than this. They come to say that our creator, that Rainbow Serpent, she get weak with anger and grief for what we are doing to this earth.

But here now you fullas. You come sit down by my fire. Warm yourselves and I will tell you the story of how this world began.

In the time of Alcheringa the land lay flat and cold. The world, she empty. The Rainbow Serpent, she asleep under the ground with all the animal tribes in her belly waiting to be born. When it her time, she push up. She come out at the heart of my people—Uluru—Ayer's Rock. She look round—everywhere all dark. No light, no color. So she get very busy now. She throw the land out—make mountains and hills. She call to her Frog Tribe to come up from their sleep and she scratch their belly to make them laugh. The water they store in the bad time spill over the land making rivers and lakes. Then she throw good spirit Biami high in the sky. She tell him to help her find light.

Now Biami, he a real good fulla. He jump up high in the sky and smile down on the land. The sky lit up from his smile and we, his children, saw color and shadow. And that warm sun spirit saw himself in the shining waters. The pine trees, they burst into flower. That's his way of telling us it's time to hunt the big mullet fish. And when the wild hop trees bloom, that's his way to tell us the oysters are fat on the shores of our great sea spirit, Quandamooka.

Grow strong, Kabul, come back to your children, the mountains, the trees, and our father, the sky. Come, bring us your birds of many colors. Come back to your rivers rushing to Quandamooka. Come back to your teeming fish of a thousand colors and shapes. Kabul is the mother of us all. She is the spirit of the land—all its beauty, all its color. But there are those who see no color, who will not feel the beauty of this land—who wish only to destroy the mother and themselves. Their eyes are open but they do not see . . . Kabul, bring back the fire of knowledge to your children. Like the fire of that pretty stone in the ground. The one you call opal. The colors of the rainbow, the colors of life itself . . .

Yet it is good for all people to dream of places that are beautiful to them. Of the waters, where they sail their boats and canoes. And now it seems that with all our great machines we can travel almost anywhere. We can travel across the land at great speed. And, for some, the city with its bright lights and the music and dancing of a modern world. There is almost nothing mankind cannot do. We can hover or swoop in the air. But where would we ask our machines to take us? They have no spirit or feelings of their own. Only we can guide them to the places that have meaning for us.

That is why, like ancestors before me, I will always come back to this place to share the feeling of the land with all living things. I belong here where the spirit of the Earth Mother is strong in the land and in me. Take time you earth fullas. Let the spirit of this mighty land touch you as it touches my people.

The water is good. It carries the strength of Kabul. Now I am rested and ready for my own journey into the world. Have I helped you to rest on your way? Perhaps soon, in all our travels, we will see Kabul in the places she has made. Perhaps she will come again when the spirits of men and the spirit of this land are once more together as one.

Man-and-Kangaroo Rock
Aboriginal Myth

HE WAS GOING ALONG, he was camping. He went on, and saw a crowd of geese. He killed them and ate them all. He started off, went on, and saw honey. He ate it all. Well, he said, "I want to cut some bamboo for spears." He went, he went farther, he saw a stand of little bamboo. He said, "I don't like them. I don't want to cut these. I'll go and cut those that Bugbug Pheasant planted, that's what I'll cut." He went, he kept on going, then he settled down and put down his belongings, and went to cut bamboo for spears. "I won't go and cut many," he said, "only two. Big ones, one for kangaroos and one for fish."

He went on. On the way he speared a kangaroo, and ate it all. Still he kept going. He went, crossed a plain there, went on a bit farther, and camped. He looked at the place and said, "I don't like *this* way, I'll go *that* way, north!" He went on, he camped, he went on, a long way.

Well then, still going on, he came to where a big sea was running. He began to swim. And after him came a kangaroo he had been trying to kill. It came running. He was swimming, swimming, but he was an old man. He kept on swimming, but the kangaroo and a dog came chasing after him where he was swimming and swimming. The dog came running close to the water's edge, and the kangaroo still went on running near where that man was swimming. The kangaroo kept running, climbed up on to the man's head, and made him sink down under the water. That man still stands there, below the surface of the sea, with the kangaroo on top of his head.

The name of the place is Neya-raingu, Wildman River. They stand there together, man and kangaroo. Let nobody go near them, where they "made themselves wrong," because it is a taboo, dangerous place always. If any new, living person goes paddling near them, a great wave might sink the canoe and everyone in it so that they drown, because it is always a taboo, dangerous place. So, people are afraid, they do not go near there, where those two "made themselves wrong." It is always taboo and dangerous. [At that place a rock stands in the open sea, in the middle of the water, with strong currents flowing around it.]

His Country—After All

Henry Lawson

THE BLENHEIM COACH was descending into the valley of the Avetere River—pronounced Aveterry—from the saddle of Taylor's Pass. Across the river to the right, the gray slopes and flats stretched away to the distant sea from a range of tussock hills. There was no native bush there; but there were several groves of imported timber standing wide apart—sentinel-like—seeming lonely and striking in their isolation.

"Grand country, New Zealand, eh?" said a stout man with a brown face, gray beard, and gray eyes, who sat between the driver and another passenger on the box.

"You don't call this grand country!" exclaimed the other passenger, who claimed to be, and looked like, a professional commercial traveler, and might have been a spieler—quite possibly both. "Why, it's about the poorest country in New Zealand! You ought to see some of the country in the North Island—Wairarapa and Napier districts, round about Pahiatua. I call this poor country."

"Well, I reckon you wouldn't, if you'd ever been in Australia—back in New South Wales. The people here don't seem to know what a grand country they've got. You say this is the worst, eh? Well, this would make an Australian cockatoo's mouth water—the worst of New Zealand would."

"I always thought Australia was all good country," mused the driver—a flax-stick. "I always thought—"

"Good country!" exclaimed the man with the gray beard, in a tone of disgust. "Why, it's only a mongrel desert, except some bits round the coast. The worst dried-up country I was ever in."

There was a silence, thoughtful on the driver's part, and aggressive on that of the stranger.

"I always thought," said the driver, reflectively, after the pause—"I always thought Australia was a good country," and he placed his foot on the brake.

They let him think. The coach descended the natural terraces above the river bank, and pulled up at the pub.

"So you're a native of Australia?" said the bagman to the gray-beard, as the coach went on again.

"Well, I suppose I am. Anyway, I was born there. That's the main thing I've got against the darned country."

"How long did you stay there?"

"Till I got away," said the stranger. Then, after a think, he added, "I went away first when I was thirty-five—went to the islands. I swore I'd never go back to Australia again; but I did. I thought I had a kind of affection for old Sydney. I knocked about the country for five or six years, and then I cleared out to Frisco. I swore I'd never go back again, and I never will."

"But surely you'll take a run over and have a look at old Sydney and those places, before you go back to America, after getting so near?"

"What the blazes do I want to have a look at the blamed country for?" snapped the stranger, who had refreshed considerably. "I've got nothing to thank Australia for—except getting out of it. It's the best country to get out of that I was ever in."

"Oh, well, I only thought you might have had some friends over there," interposed the traveler in an injured tone.

"Friends! That's another reason. I wouldn't go back there for all the friends and relations since Adam. I had more than quite enough of it while I was there. The worst and hardest years of my life were spent in Australia. I might have starved there, and did do it half my time. I worked harder and got less in my own country in five years than I ever did in any other in fifteen"—he was getting mixed— "and I've been in a few since then. No, Australia is the worst country that ever the Lord had the sense to forget. I mean to stick to the country that stuck to me, when I was starved out of my own dear native land—and that country is the United States of America. What's Australia? A big, thirsty, hungry wilderness, with one or two cities for the convenience of foreign speculators, and a few collections of humpies, called towns—also for the convenience of foreign speculators; and populated mostly by mongrel sheep, and partly by fools, who live like European slaves in the town, and like dingoes in the bush—who drivel about 'democracy,' and yet haven't any more spunk than to graft for a few Cockney dudes that razzle-dazzle most of the time in Paris. Why, the Australians haven't even got the grit to claim enough of their own money to throw a few dams across their watercourses, and so make some of the interior fit to live in. America's bad enough, but it was never so small as that. . . . Bah! The curse of Australia is sheep, and the Australian war cry is Baa!"

"Well, you're the first man I ever heard talk as you've been doing about his own country," said the bagman, getting tired and impatient of being sat on all the time. "'Lives there a man with a soul so dead, who never said—to—to himself' . . . I forget the darned thing."

He tried to remember it. The man whose soul was dead cleared his throat for action, and the driver—for whom the bagman had shouted twice as against the stranger's once—took the opportunity to observe that he always thought a man ought to stick up for his own country.

The stranger ignored him and opened fire on the bagman. He proceeded to prove that that was all rot—that patriotism was the greatest curse on earth; that it had been the cause of all war; that it was the false, ignorant sentiment that moved men to slave, starve, and fight for the comfort of their sluggish masters; that it was the enemy of universal brotherhood, the mother of hatred, murder, and slavery, and that the world would never be any better until the deadly poison, called the sentiment of patriotism, had been "educated" out of the stomachs of the people. "Patriotism!" he exclaimed scornfully. "My country! The darned fools; the country never belonged to them, but to the speculators, the absentees, land-boomers, swindlers, gangs of thieves—the men the patriotic fools starve and fight for—their masters. Ba-a!"

The opposition collapsed.

The coach had climbed the terraces on the south side of the river, and was bowling along on a level stretch of road across the elevated flat.

"What trees are those?" asked the stranger, breaking the

aggressive silence that followed his unpatriotic argument, and pointing to a grove ahead by the roadside. "They look as if they've been planted there. There ain't been a forest here surely?"

"Oh, they're some trees the Government imported," said the bagman, whose knowledge on the subject was limited. "Our own bush won't grow in this soil."

"But it looks as if anything else would—"

Here the stranger sniffed once by accident, and then several times with interest. It was a warm morning after rain. He fixed his eyes on those trees.

They didn't look like Australian gums; they tapered to the tops, the branches were pretty regular, and the boughs hung in shipshape fashion. There was not the Australian heat to twist the branches and turn the leaves.

"Why!" exclaimed the stranger, still staring and sniffing hard. "Why, dang me if they ain't (sniff) Australian gums!"

"Yes," said the driver, flicking his horses, "they are."

"Blanky (sniff) blanky old Australian gums!" exclaimed the ex-Australian, with strange enthusiasm.

"They're not old," said the driver; "they're only young trees. But they say they don't grow like that in Australia— 'count of the difference in the climate. I always thought—"

But the other did not appear to hear him; he kept staring hard at the trees they were passing. They had been planted in rows and cross-rows, and were coming on grandly.

There was a rabbit trapper's camp among those trees; he had made a fire to boil his billy with gum leaves and twigs, and it was the scent of that fire that interested the exile's nose, and brought a wave of memories with it.

"Good day, mate!" he shouted suddenly to the rabbit trapper, and to the astonishment of his fellow passengers.

"Good day, mate!" The answer came back like an echo— it seemed to him—from the past.

Presently he caught sight of a few trees that had evidently been planted before the others—as an experiment, perhaps —and, somehow, one of them had grown after its own erratic native fashion—gnarled and twisted and ragged, and could not be mistaken for anything else but an Australian gum.

"A thunderin' old blue-gum!" ejaculated the traveler, regarding the tree with great interest.

He screwed his neck to get a last glimpse, and then sat silently smoking and gazing straight ahead, as if the past lay before him—and it *was* before him.

"Ah, well!" he said, in explanation of a long meditative silence on his part; "ah, well—them saplings—the smell of them gum leaves set me thinking." And he thought some more.

"Well, for my part," said a tourist in the coach, presently, in a condescending tone, "I can't see much in Australia. The bally colonies are—"

"Oh, that be darned!" snarled the Australian-born—they had finished the second flask of whiskey. "What do you Britishers know about Australia? She's as good as England, anyway."

"Well, I suppose you'll go straight back to the States as soon as you've done your business in Christchurch," said the bagman, when near their journey's end they had become confidential.

"Well, I dunno. I reckon I'll just take a run over to Australia first. There's an old mate of mine in business in Sydney, and I'd like to have a yarn with him."

The First Gathering

Eleanor Dark

IT WAS VERY HOT, even in the shade of the trees, though indeed this shade was not unlike English shade, dense and dark and cool. The high, sparse leaves only filtered the fierce sunlight, spilling it in flickering coins of light on the bark- and twig-besprinkled ground. Mr. Johnson's voice rose and fell in a monotonous chant, and Captain Tench stifled a yawn and blinked the tears from his eyes, thinking that, in their present situation, *What shall I render to the Lord for all His benefits toward me?* was perhaps as unsuitable a text as that worthy gentleman could have chosen.

Nevertheless, he admitted, looking round with benign approval, nearly everyone was listening with a praiseworthy semblance of attention. It would be impossible to swear, for instance, from the Governor's decorously impassive face that he was wrestling mentally with the thousand problems that beset him; or from the far-away stare of Dawes that he was engrossed in calculations; or from the dark and hand-somely saturnine countenance of Hunter that he was still speculating about the natives, whose manners and customs had so intrigued his attention. Nor was the scowl on Major Ross's face to be necessarily attributed to regrets for his five fine sheep, killed yesterday by lightning, for a scowl was, nowadays, his normal expression. All one could be certain of, Tench decided, allowing his gaze to rest for a distasteful moment on the slightly open mouth and the glazing eyes of Lieutenant Clark, was that that young man's thoughts were certainly with his wife, Betsey, tales of whose peerless loveliness and impregnable virtue Captain Tench found extremely tedious.

Several of the convicts were nodding. As the service progressed and the sun beat down still more fiercely, steam rose from the ground sodden by the fierce thunderstorms of the previous two days. The Rev. Mr. Johnson, gasping in the humid air, strove manfully with his enumeration of the benefits that the Lord had rendered them, while on the western hillside Bennilong and his companions lay hidden, watching him with awe and wonder.

Was there, they marveled, no end to the eccentricities of this tribe? For now it would appear that not the slender man in the blue coat was the leader, but this other with the round, pale face like Yenandah, the moon, for all bowed their heads before him and muttered spells to avert his anger. Yet it could be seen that sometimes he lifted his face toward the sky as if in supplication, and once, his voice growing stern, he pointed, warningly, heavenward. Was it possible, Kuurinn whispered to Bennilong, that this tribe also knew of Baiame, the Good Spirit who dwells in the heavens? Might it be that the moon-faced one was aware of the visits that Baiame sometimes paid to the earth, bringing gifts to the good, and meting out punishment to the wicked, and might he, perhaps, be warning his people of such a coming, bidding them search their hearts that they might be ready to meet the judgment of the Maker-of-all?

Indeed, had his words been comprehensible to them, they might have understood him to be saying exactly that. But the convicts, to whom his exhortation was mainly addressed, were not really listening. They heard his voice only as a familiar noise, long since shorn of any meaning or of any true bearing upon their lives. "Be just," religion said to them, sheltering in the skirts of the society that meted out injustice. "Steal not," leaving them to a life in which not to steal was not to eat. "Be temperate, be continent," it said to them whose harsh existence was only made endurable by spells of black oblivion.

So they had long ago ceased to listen. They did not listen now but stood, a shuffling, ill-smelling crowd, soporific in the moist heat, thinking vaguely of scenes whose squalor stank against the primitive cleanliness of their present surroundings. Thinking of crowded city slums, of thatched hovels in the country, of a land that had repudiated them, but to which, because it was familiar, their thoughts returned with a hopeless longing. Under this torrent of hot, golden light they stood bemused, and dreamed of a gently tinted landscape. The apparent passivity of the country had not prepared them for the fury of the storm that it had loosed on them in the height of their disembarkation. The rain had come down, not in drops, but solidly; they staggered under it. It lashed their faces, ran in rivers round their ankles, soaked their ragged clothes, beat their tents and their miserable mud huts to the ground. Their nerves still remembered the horrifying sound of a great tree splintering to fragments, their eyes were wearied by the glare of lightning, their ear-drums battered to exhaustion by the crash of thunder. So now, lulled by Mr. Johnson's voice, they searched their memories for rain that fell softly, soak-

ing into green fields, splashing on stone pavements, blur-
ring the hard edges of buildings, dimming the distant hills.
These images were not thoughts, for all their thoughts were
bitter, twisted away from beauty, hardened against hope.
They were no more than a shield unconsciously set up
between themselves and an alien environment, a respite
from the effort of adjustment.

It was that word "adjustment" that was in the Governor's
mind. Looking over the ranks of convicts, he felt a bitter
indignation stir in him. He had asked for men who had
some training or some knowledge that would make them
useful in the establishment of a colony; at the very least, he
had urged, let him have sound men—healthy men. Never,
by one word, spoken or written, would he criticize His
Majesty's Government, but in his heart he knew that its
first concern had been to rid itself as expeditiously as possible of human beings whose utter uselessness would make
them, in any community, an expensive embarrassment, a
well-nigh insoluble problem.

There they were. Old, sick, idle, depraved, ignorant. His
material. On that treacherous foundation he must, somehow, build solidly. It seemed possible to him. Calm and
unemotional as he was, he could see visions. It was this
quality in him, perhaps, that had so antagonized Major
Ross, who could see little but grievances. In the lean years
still mercifully hidden from them, it was a quality that was
to sustain not only himself but the whole community. But
already he had received unfavorable accounts of the timber,
and among all the convicts he had only been able to muster
twelve carpenters, several of whom were unfit to work.
From the ships, he planned, deaf to Mr. Johnson's elo-

quence, he would hire a few more, and, lacking proper over-
seers, the marines would have to be pressed into service as
supervisors. The tools and implements that had been sent
out satisfied him neither in quantity nor in quality, but they
must be made to do. The reserve of clothing provided for
the convicts was inferior and too small; the crease between
his eyes deepened as he thought of the coming winter. He
decided, too, that he must protest again in his dispatches,
as he had protested before their departure from England,
against the incredible folly of sending convicts and stores in
different ships. In spite of the heat, he felt a cold pricking
of his skin at the thought of their plight now, had one of
their store-ships been lost on the voyage.

For it was pretty clear, already, that the country was not
going to help them to food any more than to shelter. There
seemed to be no edible fruits, few berries, and very little
game. Fish were sometimes fairly plentiful and sometimes
very scarce. The soil, too, looked less promising for cultiva-
tion than he had hoped, and he had been concerned to find
himself even poorer in agriculturists than in carpenters. In
all the colony there seemed to be not even a trained and
intelligent gardener.

In a momentary retreat from the mounting burden of his
anxieties, he thought of the land itself. Even in the turmoil
of these first days he had been conscious of a thousand new
things—strange plants, flowers, trees, seeds—things that he
had handled, examined, wondered over, wishing himself a
botanist, or that he had someone with him to take an expert
and knowledgeable interest in this treasure trove. Sir Joseph
Banks, he reflected, must see specimens of all these things.
In the course of those expeditions inland, which he was

already impatient to begin, he would make a collection to send to his friend at the first opportunity. In their unfamiliar shapes and textures they embodied, for him, the thing that he felt set against him—the almost terrifying differentness of the land. He was conscious of this, but not of his own reaction to it, and still less of the hidden significance of that reaction. For his thoughts were again of adjustment. Mr. Johnson was already adjusting himself to Divine Service beneath a tree instead of a roof. Major Ross and his marines must adjust themselves to the idea of performing duties not normally a part of their routine. The convicts, bred to see themselves as enemies of society, must be taught differently. He himself must be all the time alert to catch the mood of changing time and circumstance. He thought of it as a voluntary adjustment, not conscious of it as the first molding process of the land.

Dingo's Picnic
B. Wongar

NO DINGO EVER BARKS to express grief. We all howl. The whites never ask why, nor does Bungawa, the bishop. He stays in front of us: "Let's try it again," his hand rising up swaying a baton.

Behind Bungawa a whole mob of whites watches us. The whites have come up to St. Mary's Reserve. "Every man and his dog is here," Mr. Dogoody says loudly.

"You mean 'dingo,'" he is corrected by Verger, but does not seem to hear it, and with pipe in mouth mumbles to Bungawa: "I like your leading voice, Your Grace."

Bungawa smiles, showing a row of his metal teeth: "Every flock has a leader." While he talks he still keeps swaying that baton in front of us.

I have never seen all of us so well-groomed and gathered together, ever since that day they grouped us at *nongaru* for initiation. That was at Malag, our tribal country, and a whole world away from here.

Bungawa halts the baton for a while to give his hand a rest: "The girls will howl the National Anthem next." The mob seems pleased; Dogoody places the pipe in his mouth to free his hands, claps, then hastens the others to do the same—even Verger, Bungawa's friend, is busy with his hands.

They brought us here for a reunion picnic, every Malag soul is here, groomed and washed as never before. I had my nails cut yesterday, and a moment ago, just before they lined us up in the shade of a holly tree, Verger ran a comb through my hair: "Don't spoil the day with those fits of yours." He need not have worried—I doubt the mob would notice if I fell down. They are after our howling, not my fits, and everyone seems to be charmed by that leading voice. Dogoody has stopped clapping and says: "Jolly good!"

"It's just a rehearsal," explains Verger.

"You must have listened to these voices often when you were in the bush?"

"They sang no hymns then. It's all His Grace's idea to get them into a choir."

They have brought Bungawa a cup of tea but he is busy with us; he has selected one voice and hastens it. The howling, drawn-out and long, bounces from the tree branches and floats over the bushes in the reserve—St. Mary's is small, hardly a voice long and a throw of a boomerang across, but it is in the bush; here the howls would fly over the tops of gum trees from one end of Malag country to another and be heard by every tribal soul.

"That leading voice—whose girl is that?" Dogoody mumbles over his pipe.

Each of us has a plate hanging from the collar with a name written on it—not the one we had in the bush, but a new name that would sound pleasingly mellow to the whites. "I'd like to meet her after the rehearsal." He might be in for a surprise, perhaps not such a surprise as Bungawa when he finds out.

Bungawa glances back and smiles showing a row of teeth, but that is his way of showing that he is annoyed by the chatter. I doubt he has ever been pleased by Dogoody. The man is from his congregation and after every Sunday mass stays down at the church the whole afternoon to chat with us. I was told to shake hands with him each time we meet. He often gazes at my paw: "Different indeed—dingoes have little stumpy fingers instead of a plain pad as our mangroves have." I once sniffed a leg of his trousers and almost choked on the acrid smell of tobacco. The man places a pipe in his mouth and pats me with his free hand: "She wouldn't be right for me. Those epileptic fits, are they contagious?" The pipe must have felt loose, he tries to grip it with his lips but it slips out. "That Marngit, the witch doctor, must have cast a spell on her—the devil twisted her soul." Dogoody picks up his pipe and rubs it against my fur to wipe the dust caught on it from the ground. "Let's hope you'll find a home for her."

Bungawa halts for a while to have tea and tells us not to disperse. Dogoody steps closer and smiles: "Good old missionary zeal is back, I see."

"I'm glad you like our choir."

"You have them all in it, even that girl from the presbytery sounds great."

They look toward us again. I feel somewhat dizzy and ... the fits are hard to predict, they can strike like lightning though sometimes they creep on for days. Often it all happens so suddenly and I know of it only after I wake up—it is like coming out from a monstrous dream, my tongue all bitten and the skin bruised. That should all be over once I am back in the bush again.

Dogoody is still smiling: "Jolly good. Your Grace, you're

making history again just like when you wangled that deal with Marngit up in the bush."

Bungawa rattles his teeth, one of them must be loose, or he makes it sound that way to show that he is annoyed. When in the bush he told Marngit that those metal teeth never wear out, they are like a hatchet—sharp and tough, they could last for ever. Even after a man dies he would still keep them to crunch *ngadu,* cycad palm nut, out at our spirit world and . . . you never need to sharpen them.

Dogoody hands out a cup of tea to Bungawa: "I could have set up a table inside if that 'virgin' hut was still about."

"You mean 'dormitory,'" the teeth clatter again.

Hardly anything is left of the old St. Mary Mission but a pile of stones to boil a billy on and this old holly tree. The tree used to be evergreen in the middle of the Dry when everything else withered, because Jesus, the white man's boss, sneaked in at night and watered it, so we were told. It grew in front of the single-roomed hut we all stayed in after being brought down from *nongaru* and had to wait till Bungawa found homes for each of us. The men come out to St. Mary's for Sunday Mass, and no one talks about picnics then. We all waited, washed and clothed before being lined up under the holly tree. Each Sunday one or two of us left, but Verger kept telling us, "The world will never run out of decent bachelors."

My knees have grown numb. I'd better try and hold on a bit longer; as soon as the picnic is over I will be off to the bush and never feel fits again. It is the white man's curse, not ours, and at Malag no soul had ever been troubled with that, if it had Marngit would find the cure.

Dogoody looks at Verger now: "That leading voice girl—have you found out to whom she belongs?"

"She has no tag?"

"Don't tell me she's a stray."

Verger whispers: "She's one of them for sure—might have come to the reunion on her own."

Why do they think it has to be a girl? It would not matter to Bungawa who it is as long as it is a Malag soul and howls well. For how long will Bungawa carry on with this rehearsal? The sun has grown pitilessly hot. The holly has long ago lost most of its leaves and scattered them; the few that still remain have turned yellow and withered. Pity there is no shade to shelter in; the ants must have hollowed inside the trunk of that tree, and will soon finish that too, as they did the hut. The corrugated sheets of the hut's roof were actually eaten by the rust. The place was always too hot to be able to rest anywhere. We all sat under the holly day and night; when laden with leaves the tree sheltered you, from whatever world one might come.

Dogoody sucks his pipe: "That fellow Marngit, he'd have been pleased to see his girls in the choir. Has he been invited?"

"They're not his—all converted the day we brought them."

Dogoody took the pipe out of his mouth: "You told me before they were seized from the ceremonial ground."

Verger grins: "It was a business deal between His Grace and Marngit."

Dogoody mumbles something; he used to be told often of the story how they got us from the bush, but hardly believed any of it. He used to come to the St. Mary Mission every Sunday, and sitting with Verger on the verandah of the hut would mumble: "Nice bunch of gins. How about a couple?" He was told that only one of us would be given to each man, but he complained of Bungawa being too mean: "He got a whole tribe of them for nothing."

Verger tried to explain: "It was a proper trade—each girl would be given to a Christian home. No bigamy, His Grace says."

Dogoody chose me, but on finding out about my fits came back several days later very cross: "Bloody epileptic—take her back to that witch doctor and ask for a refund."

Now, many years later, his voice has mellowed: "I hope you have invited that tribal healer from the bush."

We are howling "Waltzing Matilda" now—Marngit, our leading voice, is asked to sound it out alone. Verger was about to say something but holds on to hear the tune. I doubt he would know to whom the voice belonged, but he likes the song. When in our country he used to whistle "Waltzing Matilda" often and tried to teach Marngit to do so too. So keen was he, that he persisted with it for years, always showing our medicine man how to hold his lips and tongue, but how could a toothless man whistle? Perhaps the whites never grew that way to understand it, we all thought.

Across the reserve echoes the single howl; yes, it is Marngit all right. Bungawa keeps swaying the baton to hasten him, but I doubt the white man can keep it up for long—he halts for a moment to wipe his eyebrows soaked with sweat.

"Jolly good," Dogoody whispers to Verger. "You'll introduce me to her."

"You have to ask His Grace."

"She must be staying down at the presbytery with all of yours."

"I have never seen her before."

The whites know little about our souls, let alone Marngit and his magic. The medicine man can turn into any being or shape if he has to. Bungawa might find that out soon, but by then I will be on my way, led back to our tribal country.

Bungawa wipes his forehead again; perhaps he likes to see how long one can howl. Our spirits howl much longer than humans could last. Marngit might never have told him that. Up at Malag, the medicine man often sat under a *wiwar*, she-oak, crushing *ngadu* with stones; Bungawa called to see him every day and was always given a handful of nuts. The white always clattered with his metal teeth while he ate the food. The two elders hardly chatted much, but Marngit liked to watch him eating and hardly blinked as though not to disturb the munching sound. They sat together throughout the day and followed *wiwar* shade as it moved around. They say that the white man was given those metal teeth by Jesus, his spiritual ancestor and the same fellow who made the first hatchet. The day the white man came to Malag, one of those hatchets was given to Marngit to chop *ngadu*, though he would have been much happier with a set of metal teeth.

The fits will be here soon—a willy-willy whirls in my head. If I swing backward I can lean on Marngit. No, he would not mind, he has come a long way to fetch me. Last night he called in my dream to tell me all about it: "They want you back with us," he looked just as I saw him last in the bush—only one tooth left in both of his jaws.

That man Dogoody is still talking: "What about a deal. Look, if I am given that howling beauty . . ."

"I doubt His Grace will part with that one."

"With the beauty, I'll take that epileptic girl as well."

"His Grace prefers making history to deals."

Jesus decided to give Marngit teeth but he wanted to have a gift from our tribe first, Bungawa told our medicine man. He was then invited to *nongaru* to take part in the initiation ceremony, to choose as many young girls as he liked and take them to his boss. The tribal elders did not like that; no white man has ever seen our initiation ceremony before, but they did not spoil the deal—the white man brought the first hatchet to Malag and it looked now that metal teeth were on the way—who could have cursed that?

The howling is over at last. "Back to your master, each of of you," Bungawa tells us. Marngit stays on though and hangs on to him. He looks his best today—shiny fur and bushy tail, a stripe rings each of his front limbs below the ankle. Is it instead of wearing a headband to show the rest of us that he is not just a dingo?

The dingo was our tribal ancestor and the one who made Malag country and brought about the tribe. That was in the Dreaming, the beginning of the black man's world. A monster came from the sea then in an immense storm followed by a flood that dragged away every tribal soul. The ancestor survived by crawling into a hollow log and drifting over the flooded country to the hills. His young wife had disappeared too; he tried to make a fire at a rock shelter, but the wood sticks were wet. He rubbed them for days with palms covered by blisters, his fingers grew stumpy from the wounds and the hands became paws. He turned into a dingo and howled toward the sea calling for his young wife to come back and make the fire.

Bungawa's hand stretches out to scratch Marngit behind

the ears—Marngit feels embarrassed at being cuddled and yawns, or maybe he does it to show that now, as a young dingo, he has all his teeth back, both jaws of them—tough and sharp they look. I doubt Verger likes the sight of the open jaws and asks, "Your Grace, shall I put a muzzle on her?"

"It's safe—I can tell when I'm loved." Bungawa speaks of love more than any other man, white or black. That deal he made with Marngit, it was: "For the love of Jesus," he said when in the bush, and instead of selecting a few girls he took all of us away from *nongaru* for his boss, though he promised Marngit to send back any of us who would not be wanted. Poor Marngit, he never got his metal teeth. He might do that now though; he has already taken Bungawa for a walk. They walked off side by side, as though strolling under *wiwar* trees at Malag, went past the old mission place and disappeared behind the bushes further on down the reserve. That was a while ago, but Dogoody is still looking toward there: "He whisked away the stray."

"They just went for a stroll—should be back soon."

Verger should know that Bungawa and Marngit are never in a hurry. They will look around for a deep shade and might rest there till the sun is down, just like at Malag in the old days.

Dogoody sucks on his empty pipe: "It looks like you'll be stuck with that epileptic for ever."

"She's going back, has been waiting for years for them to come and claim her."

"Who will come?"

"Marngit, I reckon. She was promised to the old fellow to look after him. He could not live on nuts alone, even with a good hatchet to crack them. His Grace thought he heard him howling at night from the far bush. It might . . ."

The world went away suddenly and then came back slowly. I am lying among the bushes now; my hands still grip the ground though the fits have gone. The men might not have noticed that I had a fit—they have been busy with Bungawa. They dragged him out from behind the bushes and laid his body stretched out in the shade of the holly tree. One of his hands stands up in the air as though still trying to hasten our howling. Verger forces that hand to lie on the chest: "It must have been quite a stroke to knock him off suddenly like this." The hand has grown stiff but it springs up from the chest again. His mouth is open, he looks hollow.

"His heart gave up so easily."

"He never suffered from it before."

"Too much excitement, I reckon. That stray must have shot through." No pipe is visible either in Dogoody's hands or mouth—no time to fiddle with it when you struggle with a dead fellow.

Do the whites see that Bungawa is left without his metal teeth? Perhaps they know it, but you do not need them in the white man's spirit world, for Jesus is there to make you new ones. Our world is different though, and Marngit had to come all the way and claim them. He had left in a hurry but will be back tomorrow or the day after to take me away. When I am with him I can grind the nuts on the stones, make the fire and dig pits in the sand by the fire for him to rest. Old men are like dingoes. They will howl for you if left alone.

At the Source of Life

Arthur Upfield

SUMMER'S FIRST HEAT WAVE found Dot and Dash at Carr's Tank, twenty-two miles south of Range Hut, and lying at the west foot of the ranges. The tank was a great square earth excavation from which thirty thousand cubic yards of mullock had been taken by bullock-drawn scoops. The mullock formed a rampart, and through this rampart cement pipes conducted the water from a shallow creek—when water flowed in it—beginning in the hills.

Wholly enclosing tank and banks was a six-wire fence, but so numerous were the kangaroos that hardly one strand of wire remained taut. With no difficulty whatsoever they climbed through the fence to drink at the dam in preference to drinking at the man-made sheep trough a hundred yards out, and kept filled by a windmill.

Still farther away was an erection of corrugated iron, hessian bags, and flattened petrol tins, which served as a kind of house for two stockmen. This sort of house substitute was less in evidence on Windee than on the great majority of Australian stations. There exists an act that requires the squatter to house his men in enlarged iron boxes, also an act requiring him to use poison-carts to destroy rabbits. However, since no one lives in the bush with the intention of settling there, but rather to make a check and then settle elsewhere, the want of any degree of comfort is a matter of indifference.

The two stockmen and the partners were having an early dinner, since the latter had to be at their places at the dam before sundown. In spite of the terrific heat in the interior of the hut the four men appeared to enjoy eating, seeming hardly conscious of the perspiration that ran from them, brought out by the scalding-hot tea drunk from tin pint pannikins. The wind, gusty and hot, rattled the iron sheets nailed to the framework of the structure, and sometimes thickened the atmosphere with fine red dust. Countless flies hummed and settled in eyes and on bare necks and arms. That day the temperature in the shade at Windee was from 102° to 112°. At Carr's Tank there was no shade much for a distance of fully a mile in any direction.

"Feeling a bit warm, Dot?" queried Ned Swallow, a youthful, lank, red-headed rider.

"Not exactly," Dot rejoined, helping himself to what purported to be plum duff. 'I was jest wonderin' whar the draught was coming from. Say, Tom!"—to the second rider —"you sure can make plum duff!"

"That's a better pudding than general," Tom growled.

"Well, it's fillin', anyway. Try some, Dash?"

"I think not," Dash said, eyeing it suspiciously.

"Seems as though the outside third of it kinda got stuck on the cloth when you heaved her out, Tom," Dot observed.

"Yus. I forgot to wet the cloth afore I put her in. Still, it'll

go better cold. She'll have lost that slummicky look. Don't
you blokes wait to wash up. Me and Ned'll do that."

"You are very decent, Tom. I'll roll a cigarette and Dot
and I will adjourn." Dash went outside and dried his face,
neck, and arms with a towel. The sun was getting low, and
already thousands of galahs whirled about the tank, or
strutted on the banks looking like tiny gray-coated soldiers.
Around the tank lay a plain covered with fine red dust. One
mile away the scrub began. Before the tank was sunk, all
that plain bore scrub trees, but by now the stock converging there daily had eaten or killed them. Across this arid
desert drifted an occasional low cloud of red dust, while at
a point far to the northwest, a huge towering red column
denoted that the sheep were coming in to drink.

Dash settled himself at the summit of the rampart at that
angle that commanded the iron reservoir tanks, windmill,
and troughs giving water to two paddocks, with a great
sweep of the plain beyond; while Dot, at the opposite angle,
commanded the shorter stretch of plain bounded by the
range.

As a slowly oncoming destroyer sending up a red smoke
screen, a long line of sheep moved across the plain to the
dam. Shadows of tank and windmill lengthened with mag-
ical rapidity, and the wind became merely a fitful zephyr.

The red dust screen came ever nearer. Dash could observe
the faint white figures of the leaders of the flock of three
thousand sheep. On his side Dot could see a similar flock
of sheep coming from the other paddock to drink. A mile
away three black pinheads behaved as well-drilled jumping
fleas, and between each jump a spurt of dust arose. They

were the vanguard of the kangaroos coming leisurely to the dam in fifteen-foot jumps, tireless, wonderfully speedy, infinitely more graceful in action than a racing horse or whippet dog. At the edge of the scrub numbers of these animals, who had slept and drowsed away the day, were sitting bolt upright watching their leaders, and in twos and threes and fours they bounded out on the plain, so that a few minutes after Dash had seen the first three pinheads he could easily count thirty.

Water! The Spring of Life!

The nearest water lay eighteen miles to the north; the next nearest thirty miles to the west. Between these places the only moisture to be found was in the sap of the trees. In a week or so, when the last of the tiny grass roots were dead, twenty to fifty thousand rabbits would come to water every night with unfailing regularity. Numbers of them even then were drinking at the edges of the square sheet of water in the dam. Others were converging on it in easy stages of a few yards' run, with pauses to sit up and look around with alert suspicion.

When the sun, still fiercely hot and flaming red, was but four fingers above the horizon, the dust cloud was within a quarter of a mile of the troughs. Fifty sheep were to be seen moving at its base. Tens of hundreds walked in the cloud in several parallel lines. Dash could hear their plaintive baaing above the scream of the birds, and he observed with never-slackening interest how but one sheep of all that great flock constituted itself the leader. It was an old yet robust ewe. When but a hundred yards from the troughs she broke into a quick amble, followed by those immediately behind her.

That seemed to be the point when every following sheep broke from a walk into a run.

A white flood of wool rolled over the ground to the water. The galahs rose from the troughs with a thunderous roar of wings to fly a short distance away and settle like a gray blanket on the expanse of plain. The white flood, reaching the trough, poured around both sides of it and rolled outward as from a center when the main body of the sheep swelled its volume.

A vast milling, dust-raising, baaing, struggling mass of animals! The level of water in the reservoir tank feeding the trough began gradually to fall. Then from the surging mass one sheep became detached. It was the old ewe leader. She ran back over the way she had come, followed by several others, and then stopped when two hundred yards from the tank, looking back with cunning placidity. In twos and threes, their bellies distended with water, sheep left the mob and joined her, then, with her, to stand awhile looking back. Not one ran ahead. And not before all but a few lingerers had drunk their fill did she lead them out across the plain to the scrub and dry grass, the red mounting dust, now rising straight and to a great height, marking their passage.

The army corps of galahs was retreating by battalions to roosting places in the mulga trees on the hills. A thunder of hoofs caused Dash to look to his left and observe the second flock of sheep—also led by a single animal—charge in and around the second trough. When they also had gone the sun was set and Dash lay with his .22 Savage resting in his arms. There were seven kangaroos within range of his rifle, namely, three hundred yards.

Dash settled down to careful shooting while the light held. The cartridges he used cost fourpence each, so that he could not afford to miss often. Dot, firing from his .44 Winchester his own loading cartridges, the cost of which he had carefully worked out at five shillings per hundred, could well afford to take chances; but his was far less deadly beyond two hundred yards than the Savage.

His partner heard him shooting, and sometimes cursing. A quite friendly rivalry existed between them when in the morning they counted their respective bags, after which the merits of their rifles would be argued. The light began to go rapidly, and presently Dash missed for the first time that evening. His following shot was a miss; and, slipping down behind the rampart, he walked to where a single blanket was folded in its length. Beside it lay a double-barreled shotgun of beautiful workmanship, several boxes of BB size cartridges, a billy-can of cold tea, and a hurricane lamp.

It was his night position. It was situated in a right angle on the narrow strip of level ground between the bank of the dam and the rampart of mullock. In a similar position in the opposite angle lay Dot. Each of them commanded two sides of the square-shaped tank, and to shoot each other was impossible unless one fired diagonally across the water.

Lighting a cigarette, Dash lay back on the blanket resting his head on his hands. To regard him then was to wonder what form of madness had exiled him from home and country. There was no trace of dissipation on the strong sunburned face, no hint of weakness about the straight mouth and square chin.

His cigarette finished, he sat up and sipped from the blackened billy-can. Above him the sky was blue-black and the stars did not twinkle with so-called tropical brilliance, despite the fact that it was cloudless. The features of the mullock marking his zone of operations were blurred by the general shadow, but those angles of the rampart commanded by Dot still revealed the crevices among the rubble in a soft amber glow. The level summit of Dash's rampart was clear-cut against the dull pink sheen of the western sky. That skyline would be visible all night long, hence his then position.

A form, soundless in movement, grotesque, almost monstrous, slowly pushed up on that skyline. Dash reached for his shotgun. The form became still for a moment, then slowly changed from the grotesque to the beautiful, from the monstrous to the lovely, when the kangaroo sat up, his tail resting on the ground balancing him like a third leg, his small but noble head and lifted stiffened ears outlined as a clear-cut silhouette against the darkening sky.

A sharp flash, a roar, and the 'roo lay thrashing in its death agonies.

"Poor devil!" sighed Dash.

From beyond the bank a succession of twin thuds went out as warning to the converging kangaroos, when one or more gave the signal by jumping and bringing their tails down on the earth with a sound like that of a stick beating a dusty carpet.

Dot fired, and Dash heard the wounded 'roo "queex-queex" with pain and anger. Then his attention was taken by the rising figures of two 'roos directly opposite him and less than twenty yards distant. He fired twice rapidly, and both animals fell dead. Dash was thankful.

At about eleven o'clock the shooting became less frequent, and Dot at last called out for an armistice. Dash agreed, and lit his lamp. Whereupon each man dispatched his wounded animals with his hunting knife.

"How many?" Dot asked when the lights revealed both at their respective camps.

"Twenty-nine," replied Dash without enthusiasm. "What is your tally?"

"Thirty-three," came the triumphant answer.

After that, silence fell once more. The tall partner lay on his side, smoking and thinking. The air was still heated by the roasted earth. The silence became oppressive, more oppressive than the sounds of continuous thunder.

Presently the armistice was called off and hostilities were resumed till dawn.

The Chosen Vessel

Barbara Baynton

SHE LAID THE STICK and her baby on the grass while she untied the rope that tethered the calf. The length of the rope separated them. The cow was near the calf, and both were lying down. Feed along the creek was plentiful, and every day she found a fresh place to tether it, since tether it she must, for if she did not, it would stray with the cow out on the plain. She had plenty of time to go after it, but then there was her baby; and if the cow turned on her out on the plain, and she with her baby—she had been a town girl and was afraid of the cow, but she did not want the cow to know it. She used to run at first when it bellowed its protest against the penning up of its calf. This satisfied the cow, also the calf, but the woman's husband was angry and called her —the noun was cur. It was he who forced her to run and meet the advancing cow, brandishing a stick, and uttering threatening words till the enemy turned and ran. "That's the way!" the man said, laughing at her white face. In many things he was worse than the cow, and she wondered if the same rule would apply to the man, but she was not one to provoke skirmishes even with the cow.

It was early for the calf to go to "bed"—nearly an hour

earlier than usual; but she had felt so restless all day. Partly because it was Monday, and the end of the week that would bring her and the baby the companionship of his father was so far off. He was a shearer, and had gone to his shed before daylight that morning. Fifteen miles as the crow flies separated them.

There was a track in front of the house, for it had once been a wine shanty, and a few travelers passed along at intervals. She was not afraid of horsemen; but swagmen, going to, or worse coming from, the dismal, drunken little township, a day's journey beyond, terrified her. One had called at the house today, and asked for tucker.

That was why she had penned up the calf so early. She feared more from the look of his eyes, and the gleam of his teeth, as he watched her newly awakened baby beat its impatient fists upon her covered breasts, than from the knife that was sheathed in the belt at his waist.

She had given him bread and meat. Her husband, she told him, was sick. She always said that when she was alone and a swagman came; and she had gone in from the kitchen to the bedroom, and asked questions and replied to them in the best man's voice she could assume. Then he had asked to go into the kitchen to boil his billy, but instead she gave him tea, and he drank it on the wood heap. He had walked round and round the house, and there were cracks in some places, and after the last time he had asked for tobacco. She had none to give him, and he had grinned, because there was a broken clay pipe near the wood heap where he stood, and if there were a man inside, there ought to have been tobacco. Then he asked for money, but women in the bush never have money.

At last he had gone, and she, watching through the cracks, saw him, when about a quarter of a mile away, turn and look back at the house. He had stood so for some moments with a pretense of fixing his swag, and then, apparently satisfied, moved to the left toward the creek. The creek made a bow round the house, and when he came to the bend she lost sight of him. Hours after, watching intently for signs of smoke, she saw the man's dog chasing some sheep that had gone to the creek for water, and saw it slink back suddenly, as if it had been called by someone.

More than once she thought of taking her baby and going to her husband. But in the past, when she had dared to speak of the dangers to which her loneliness exposed her, he had taunted and sneered at her. "Needn't flatter yerself," he had told her, "nobody 'ud want ter run away with yew."

Long before nightfall she placed food on the kitchen table, and beside it laid the big brooch that had been her mother's. It was the only thing of value that she had. And she left the kitchen door wide open.

The doors inside she securely fastened. Beside the bolt in the back one she drove in the steel and scissors; against it she piled the table and the stools. Underneath the lock of the front door she forced the handle of the spade, and the blade between the cracks in the flooring boards. Then the prop-stick, cut into lengths, held the top, as the spade held the middle. The windows were little more than portholes; she had nothing to fear through them.

She ate a few mouthfuls of food and drank a cup of milk. But she lighted no fire, and when night came, no candle, but crept with her baby to bed.

What woke her? The wonder was that she had slept—she

had not meant to. But she was young, very young. Perhaps the shrinking of the galvanized roof—hardly though, since that was so usual. Yet something had set her heart beating wildly; but she lay quite still, only she put her arm over her baby. Then she had both round it, and she prayed, "Little baby, little baby, don't wake!"

The moon's rays shone on the front of the house, and she saw one of the open cracks, quite close to where she lay, darken with a shadow. Then a protesting growl reached her; and she could fancy she heard the man turn hastily. She plainly heard the thud of something striking the dog's ribs, and the long flying strides of the animal as it howled and ran. Still watching, she saw the shadow darken every crack along the wall. She knew by the sounds that the man was trying every standpoint that might help him to see in; but how much he saw she could not tell. She thought of many things she might do to deceive him into the idea that she was not alone. But the sound of her voice would wake baby, and she dreaded that as though it were the only danger that threatened her. So she prayed, "Little baby, don't wake, don't cry!"

Stealthily the man crept about. She knew he had his boots off, because of the vibration that his feet caused as he walked along the veranda to gauge the width of the little window in her room, and the resistance of the front door.

Then he went to the other end, and the uncertainty of what he was doing became unendurable. She had felt safer, far safer, while he was close and she could watch and listen. She felt she must watch, but the great fear of wakening her baby again assailed her. She suddenly recalled that one of the slabs on that side of the house had shrunk in length as well as in width, and had once fallen out. It was held in position only by a wedge of wood underneath. What if he should discover that? The uncertainty increased her terror. She prayed as she gently raised herself with her little one in her arms, held tightly to her breast.

She thought of the knife, and shielded the baby's body with her hands and arms. Even the little feet she covered with its white gown, and the baby never murmured—it liked to be held so. Noiselessly she crossed to the other side, and stood where she could see and hear, but not be seen. He was trying every slab, and was very near to that with the wedge under it. Then she saw him find it; and heard the sound of the knife as bit by bit he began to cut away the wooden support.

She waited motionless, with her baby pressed tightly to her, though she knew that in another few minutes this man with the cruel eyes, lascivious mouth, and gleaming knife would enter. One side of the slab tilted; he had only to cut away the remaining little end, when the slab, unless he held it, would fall outside.

She heard his jerked breathing as it kept time with the cuts of the knife, and the brush of his clothes as he rubbed the wall in his movements, for she was so still and quiet that she did not even tremble. She knew when he ceased, and wondered why, being so well concealed; for he could not see her, and would not fear if he did, yet she heard him move cautiously away. Perhaps he expected the slab to fall—his motive puzzled her, and she moved even closer, and bent her body the better to listen. Ah! what sound was that? "Listen! Listen!" she bade her heart—her heart that had kept so still, but now bounded with tumultuous throbs that dulled her ears. Nearer and nearer came the sounds, till the welcome thud of a horse's hoof rang out clearly.

"O God! O God! O God!" she panted, for they were very close before she could make sure. She rushed to the door, and with her baby in her arms tore frantically at its bolts and bars.

Out she darted at last and, running madly along, saw the horseman beyond her in the distance. She called to him in Christ's name, in her baby's name, still flying like the wind with the speed that deadly peril gives. But the distance grew greater and greater between them, and when she reached the creek her prayers turned to wild shrieks, for there crouched the man she feared, with outstretched arms that caught her as she fell. She knew he was offering terms if she ceased to struggle and cry for help, though louder and louder did she cry for it, but it was only when the man's hand gripped her throat that the cry of "Murder" came from her lips. And when she ceased, the startled curlews took up the awful sound, and flew wailing "Murder! Murder!" over the horseman's head.

"By God!" said the boundary rider, "it's been a dingo right enough! Eight killed up here, and there's more down in the creek—a ewe and a lamb, I'll bet; and the lamb's alive!" He shut out the sky with his hand, and watched the crows that were circling round and round, nearing the earth one moment, and the next shooting skyward. By that he knew the lamb must be alive; even a dingo will spare a lamb sometimes.

Yes, the lamb was alive, and after the manner of lambs of its kind did not know its mother when the light came. It had sucked the still warm breasts, and laid its little head on her bosom, and slept till the morn. Then, when it looked at the swollen disfigured face, it wept and would have crept away, but for the hand that still clutched its little gown. Sleep was nodding its golden head and swaying its small body, and the crows were close, so close, to the mother's wide-open eyes, when the boundary rider galloped down.

"Jesus Christ!" he said, covering his eyes. He told afterward how the little child held out its arms to him, and how he was forced to cut its gown that the dead hand held.

It was election time, and as usual the priest had selected a candidate. His choice was so obviously in the interests of the squatter that Peter Hennessey's reason, for once in his life, had overridden superstition, and he had dared promise his vote to another. Yet he was uneasy, and every time he woke in the night (and it was often), he heard the murmur of his mother's voice. It came through the partition, or under the door. If through the partition, he knew she was praying in her bed; but when the sounds came under the door, she was on her knees before the little altar in the corner that enshrined the statue of the Blessed Virgin and Child.

"Mary, Mother of Christ! Save my son! Save him!" prayed she in the dairy as she strained and set the evening's milking. "Sweet Mary! For the love of Christ, save him!" The grief in her old face made the morning meal so bitter that to avoid her he came late to his dinner. It made him so cowardly that he could not say good-bye to her, and when night fell on the eve of the election day, he rode off secretly.

He had thirty miles to ride to the township to record his vote. He cantered briskly along the great stretch of plain that had nothing but stunted cotton bush to play shadow to the full moon, which glorified a sky of earliest spring. The bruised incense of the flowering clover rose up to him, and the glory of the night appealed vaguely to his imagination, but he was preoccupied with his present act of revolt.

Vividly he saw his mother's agony when she would find him gone. Even at that moment, he felt sure, she was praying.

"Mary! Mother of Christ!" He repeated the invocation, half unconsciously, when suddenly to him, out of the stillness, came Christ's name—called loudly in despairing accents.

"For Christ's sake! Christ's sake! Christ's sake!" called the voice. Good Catholic that he had been, he crossed himself before he dared to look back. Gliding across a ghostly patch of pipe-clay, he saw a white-robed figure with a babe clasped to her bosom.

All the superstitious awe of his race and religion swayed his brain. The moonlight on the gleaming clay was a "heavenly light" to him, and he knew the white figure not for flesh and blood, but for the Virgin and Child of his mother's prayers. Then, good Catholic that once more he was, he put spurs to his horse's sides and galloped madly away.

His mother's prayers were answered, for Hennessey was the first to record his vote—for the priest's candidate. Then he sought the priest at home, but found that he was out rallying the voters. Still, under the influence of his blessed vision, Hennessey would not go near the public houses, but wandered about the outskirts of the town for hours, keeping apart from the townspeople, and fasting as penance. He was subdued and mildly ecstatic, feeling as a repentant chastened child, who awaits only the kiss of peace.

And at last, as he stood in the graveyard crossing himself with reverent awe, he heard in the gathering twilight the roar of many voices crying the name of the victor at the election. It was well with the priest.

Again Hennessey sought him. He was at home, the housekeeper said, and led him into the dimly lighted study. His seat was immediately opposite a large picture, and as the housekeeper turned up the lamp, once more the face of the Madonna and Child looked down on him, but this time silently, peacefully. The half-parted lips of the Virgin were smiling with compassionate tenderness; her eyes seemed to beam with the forgiveness of an earthly mother for her erring but beloved child.

He fell on his knees in adoration. Transfixed, the wondering priest stood, for mingled with the adoration, "My lord and my God!" was the exaltation, "And hast Thou chosen me?"

"What is it, Peter?" said the priest.

"Father," he answered reverently; and with loosened tongue he poured forth the story of his vision.

"Great God!" shouted the priest, "and you did not stop to save her! Do you not know? Have you not heard?"

Many miles further down the creek a man kept throwing an old cap into a water hole. The dog would bring it out and lay it on the opposite side to where the man stood, but would not allow the man to catch him, though it was only to wash the blood of the sheep from his mouth and throat, for the sight of blood made the man tremble. But the dog also was guilty.

We Embark in the Bear Industry

Steele Rudd

WHEN THE BAILIFF CAME and took away the cows and horses, and completely knocked the bottom out of Dad's land scheme, Dad didn't sit in the ashes and sulk. He wasn't that kind of person. He *did* at times say he was tired of it all, and often he wished it far enough, too! But, then, that was all mere talk on Dad's part. He *loved* the selection. To every inch—every stick of it—he was devoted. 'Twas his creed. He felt certain there was money in it—that out of it would come his independence. Therefore, he didn't roll up and, with Mother by the hand and little Bill on his back, stalk into town to hang round and abuse the Bush. He walked up and down the yard thinking and thinking. Dad was a man with a head.

He consulted Mother and Dave, and together they thought more.

"The thing is," Dad said, "to get another horse to finish the bit of plowing. We've got *one*; Anderson will lend the gray mare, I know."

He walked round the room a few times.

"When that's done, I think I see my way clear; but that's the trouble."

He looked at Dave. Dave seemed as though he had a solution. But Joe spoke.

"Kuk-kuk-couldn't y' b-reak in some kang'roos, Dad? There's pul-lenty in th' pup-paddick."

"Couldn't you shut up and hold your tongue and clear out of this, you brat?" Dad roared. And Joe hung his head and shut up.

"Well, y' know"—Dave drawled—"there's that colt wot Maloney offered us before to quieten. Could get 'im. 'E's a big lump of a 'orse if y' could do anythin' with 'im. *They* gave 'im best themselves."

Dad's eyes shone.

"That's th' horse," he cried. "*Get* him! Tomorrow first thing go for him! *I'll* make something of him!"

"Don't know"—Dave chuckled—"he's a—"

"Tut, tut; you fetch him."

"Oh, I'll *fetch* 'im." And Dave, on the strength of having made a valuable suggestion, dragged Joe off the sofa and stretched himself upon it.

Dad went on thinking awhile. "How much," he at last asked, "did Johnson get for those skins?"

"Which?" Dave answered, "Bears or kangaroos?"

"Bears."

"Five bob, wasn't it? Six for some."

"What, *apiece*?"

"Yairs."

"Why, God bless my soul, what have we been thinking about? *Five shillings*? Are you sure?"

"Yairs, rather."

"What, bearskins worth that and the paddock here and the lanes and the country overrun with them—*full* of the damn things—*hundreds* of them—and we, all this time—all these years—working and slaving and scraping and—and" (he almost shouted), "*damn* me! what asses we *have* been, to be sure." (Dave stared at him.) "Bear skins *five shillings* each, and—"

"That's right enough," Dave interrupted, "but—"

"Of *course* it's right enough *now*," Dad yelled, "now when we *see* it."

"But look!" and Dave sat up and assumed an arbitrary attitude. He was growing suspicious of Dad's ideas. "To begin with, how many bears do you reckon on getting in a day?"

"In a day"—reflectively—"twenty at the least."

"Twenty. Well, say we only got *half* that, how much d' y' make?"

"*Make*?" (considering). "Two pounds ten a day . . . fifteen or twenty pounds a week . . . yes, twenty pounds, reckoning at *that* even. And do you mean to tell me that we wouldn't get more than *ten* bears a day? Why we'd get more than that in the lane—get more up *one* tree."

Dave grinned.

"Can't you *see*? *Damn* it, boy, are you *so* dense?"

Dave saw. He became enthusiastic. He wondered why it had never struck us before. Then Dad smiled, and we sat to supper and talked about bears.

"We'll not bother with that horse *now*," said Dad; "the plowing can go; I'm *done* with it. We've had enough poking and puddling about. We'll start this business straight away." And the following morning, headed by the dog and Dad, armed with a tomahawk, we started up the paddock.

How free we felt! To think we were finished forever with

the raking and carting of hay—finished tramping up and down beside Dad, with the plow reins in our hands, flies in our eyes, and burr in our feet—finished being the target for Dad's blasphemy when the plow or the horses or the harness went wrong—was delightful! And the adventure and excitement that this new industry promised operated strongly upon us. We rioted and careered like hunted brumbies through the trees, till warned by Dad to "keep our eyes about"; then we settled down, and Joe found the first bear. It was on an ironbark tree, around the base of which we soon were clamoring.

"Up y'go!" Dad said, cheerfully helping Dave and the tomahawk into the first fork.

Dave ascended and crawled cautiously along the limb the bear was on and began to chop. *We* armed ourselves with heavy sticks and waited. The dog sat on his tail and stared and whined at the bear. The limb cracked, and Dave ceased chopping and shouted, "Look out!" We shouldered arms. The dog was in a hurry. He sprang in the air and landed on his back. But Dave had to make another nick or two. Then with a loud crack the limb parted and came sweeping down. The dog jumped to meet it. He met it, and was laid out on the grass. The bear scrambled to its feet and made off toward Bill. Bill squealed and fell backward over a log. Dad rushed in and kicked the bear up like a football. It landed near Joe. Joe's eyes shone with the hunter's lust of blood. He swung his stick for a tremendous blow—swung it mightily and high—and nearly knocked his parent's head off. When Dad had spat blood enough to make sure that he had only lost one tooth, he hunted Joe; but Joe was too fleet, as usual.

Meanwhile, the bear had run up another tree—about the

tallest gum in the paddock. Dad snapped his fingers angrily and cried: "Where the devil was the *dog*?"

"Oh, where the devil wuz the *dorg*!" Dave growled, sliding down the tree—"where th' devil wuz *you*? Where wuz the lot o' y'?"

"Ah, well!" Dad said—"there's plenty more we can get. Come along." And off we went. The dog pulled himself together and limped after us.

Bears were plentiful enough, but we wandered far before we found another on a tree that Dave could climb, and when we *did,* somehow or other the limb broke when he put his weight on it, and down he came, bear and all. Of course we were not ready, and that bear, like the other, got up another tree. But Dave didn't. He lay till Dad ran about two miles down a gully to a dam and filled his hat with muddy water and came tearing back with it empty—till Anderson and Mother came and helped to carry him home.

We didn't go out any more after bears. Dave, when he was able, went and got Maloney's colt and put him in the plow. And after he had kicked Dad and smashed all the swingle-trees about the place, and got right out of his harness a couple of times and sulked for two days, he went well enough beside Anderson's old gray mare.

And that season, when everyone else's wheat was red with rust—when Anderson and Maloney cut theirs for hay—when Johnson put a firestick in his—ours was good to see. It ripened; and the rain kept off, and we reaped two hundred bags. Salvation!

Misanthropy

Xavier Herbert

THE DIVERSION OF THE DAY was inspection of the great rough rawboned horse Misanthropy, owned by Paddy Bliss of Skinny Creek, and entered with the equine aristocracy of the land in that classic of North Australia, the Port Zodiac Hundred Guineas Handicap. He was by no means the favorite; Tom Hazzit's bay colt, The Goanna, was that; but whereas the distinctive qualities of The Goanna were attractive only to horseflesh-eyes, those of Misanthropy were so to anyone who could see a joke.

A joke. That's what Misanthropy was in the eyes of all who looked upon him but the Blisses. That's why inspecting him was the diversion of this Race Day. And part of the joke was the innocence of the Blisses; not only their innocence in believing that that great black dinosaur was a racehorse, but in being eager to show him off to the crowds that came tongue-in-cheek to see him, and in being so frank and happy in expounding his laughable history and their boundless faith in him.

Mrs. Bliss told Dr. Innards, the Clerk of Scales, and Tom Hazzit, owner of The Goanna, that they had such confidence in their idol that they had already ordered the clothes they would buy with the Hundred Guineas to attend the Champagne Dinner at which the Racing Club would entertain the owners of the winning horses; not that they cared much for Dollin' Up, she said, with a glance at her ancient faded skirt; but they could not very well go to the dinner Half Naked. And Paddy told everyone that though they had come there in Wheelbarrows, so to speak, they would be going away in Motor Cars. And the children were proud and happy as never in their lonely lives.

As long as anyone could remember, the Ginger Blisses of Skinny Creek had always had a Wonder Horse in training. It seemed to be the one aim of their lives to win the Hundred Guineas Handicap. For that they had striven in obscurity, and in poverty that was due to this all-absorbing cause, seemingly always.

Misanthropy was the first of the Skinny Creek Wonders to be entered in a race in Town. But he was not unknown. Far from it! He had two remarkable performances to his credit—one, given at the Annual Meeting at Republic Reef six months before, being an exhibition of his faculty for pig-rooting while traveling at a tremendous pace (unfortunately he had dashed across the course instead of round it); the other, given at the Railway Picnic at Caroline River a month or so later, being a demonstration of the acuteness of the homing instinct in a horse, he having then rid himself of his rider at the second furlong and made straight across country for the unguarded bread-bin back home at Skinny Creek. Therefore the officials of the Port Zodiac Racing Club, believing that he would only make a joke of their Classic, had tried to induce old Paddy to enter him in the unimportant Weight-for-Age. Paddy had insisted on the Handicap, saying that he now had him perfectly disciplined, that his pace was amazing, that—that—well, he was a Wonder Horse and bound to win.

So this day was not merely a race day to the Ginger Blisses, but the Day of All Days, which would see them come into their own.

It was generally known that the family had gone off to Mass that morning, taking Misanthropy to be blessed, and that it had turned out that he was cursed instead, because he broke free while the family were at their devotions, made his way into the presbytery, and ate the Reverend Father's breakfast. This part of the joke was touching. The crowd roared over the Wonder Horse himself, but looked a bit shamefaced when tittering over the innocence of his ragged owners.

Misanthropy was a brumby, born and bred among the wild horses that roamed the Leichhardt Tableland. The Blisses had captured him when he came to their tanks, dying of thirst, toward the end of the Dry Season before last. They claimed that he was a natural thoroughbred, a son of Baron Brothers' racing blood–stallion Mischief, who had taken a holiday among the brumbies some five or six years before. They were convinced of that. They tried to convince others by pointing out certain of his features and describing some of his manners, particularly his great stature and dislike for humankind, qualities for which the stallion Mischief was famed. Certainly he was a misanthrope. He even bit the loving hands that fed him, and would allow no one on his back but Paddy—and that not always. The Blisses described all this with pride. To his whim-horse qualities— the great splay hoofs, the humpy withers, the spavined hocks—they seemed quite blind.

So the Day of Days was come at last. But—Oh how the time dragged to the Hour! The visitors were a godsend. But when the races began at noon the visitors ceased to come. Then the Blisses felt lost; and they began to feel afraid—afraid. They lounged about their dusty ant-infested camp, sheltering from the withering sun beneath the dilapidated turn-out over which a tent fly and broken branches had been rigged, swatting flies and fidgeting, fidgeting and expounding their faith, expounding their faith to their own souls now to crush down rising doubts, expounding it to the object of their faith himself, who stood before them in his brush-built shelter stamping and maliciously snapping at flies, expounding it at the mirages flickering on the scrubby course, and at the purple peaks of the ranges near their distant home at Skinny Creek, which stood out like hopes above the wilderness—unless a race was being run, when the whole family leapt up, picked fancies from the thundering field, and roared and yelled and screamed them on to victory.

And then how the time from three o'clock to four just flew! One needed a dozen pairs of hands to do in time what must be done. Old Paddy in his haste, while getting a drop of water for Misanthropy, forgot that Mother had made a very tight fit of his silken jockey-breeches, and over bent himself and—zip!

Sprawling on a box with panting Mother at work on him behind, Paddy roared at Vincent who was frantically hunting for the spurs, at Joe who was trying to get the water-can away from the greedy Wonder, and at Bridie and Katie who were running about like hens. Their dream in becoming realized was developing into a nightmare.

And then the Hour! CLANGOR-CLANG! CLANGOR-CLANG! Calling up the horses for the Handicap. It seemed like calling up the Blisses to their doom. They found themselves entangled at the Saddling Paddock gate, struggling to kiss Father and to hold the fractious Wonder. A wrench —and they were parted. More wrenches while Paddy and Vincent hauled the Wonder through the gate. Misanthropy's ears were back, his eyes showing white, his nostrils dilated and quivering. "Look at him!" moaned Paddy. "Look at the cow! Oh my gawd he's startin'!"

CLANG!

Misanthropy jumped as though the tongue of the bell had struck him. He backed to the fence, dragging Paddy and Vincent after him. He reached the fence, lashed out, scuttled the grinning crowd, became entangled in the wires.

A burst of laughter. Paddy moaned again, and at the risk of his life freed the savage hoofs. Other hands came to help; and Misanthropy was dragged across the paddock by main force. Then Paddy took his saddle and whip and joined the procession to the Scales for the Weighing Out.

Misanthropy was listed to carry nine stone two. That made it appear on paper as though he were a likely winner, since some of the most favored horses were not carrying much more. The Blisses had felt rather flattered by this fact, believing that the weight was a handicap deliberately chosen. Actually it was a rough guess at the weight of Paddy by the Handicapper, who would have allotted Misanthropy the lowest weight in the field but for knowing that Paddy was going to ride him and that Paddy's weight was about nine stone two.

Paddy's breeches split again when he sat in the seat of the

scales. He did not know it. He was dazed. His face was beetroot-red and streaked with sweat, his brown eyes goggling, his long carroty moustaches twitching. Dr. Innards, the Clerk, handled him as though he were a patient.

Tom Hazzit, who was going to ride his own horse The Goanna and was awaiting his turn on the scales, saw the gaping rent in Paddy's breeches as Paddy blundered toward the scale-shed door. "Wait on, Paddy!" he cried.

Paddy did not hear. He was tripping on his jangling trailing stirrups. Tom Hazzit went after him and whispered. Paddy gasped and choked, while clutching at the rent and looking helplessly about. Not a smile was to be seen, though the audience was bursting.

"I'll fix it," said Dr. Innards. "Come here." He took Paddy's arm and drew him over to the ambulance-box, from which he drew a roll of lint and several safety pins. Gravely he cut off a piece of lint and pinned it inside the breeches; and when that was done he took out a glass and a bottle of brandy, and, grunting "Bit of a steadier won't hurt you," poured out a very stiff peg.

"Goo' luck," gasped Paddy as he raised the glass. "Same to you," said the doctor.

"Good old Paddy," said Hazzit.

"Go in and show 'em," said the doctor, and gently pushed him out.

"Go in and show 'em," muttered Paddy as he fought to saddle the Wonder Horse. "Go in and show 'em!" he hissed. "Go in and show 'em!" he shouted as at the sixth attempt to mount he flopped into the saddle.

Misanthropy began to buck. Paddy held him with all his might and outraged his petted ears by bawling, "Go in and show 'em—go in and win, you blanky myall—or I'll shoot ya and feed ya to the crows!"

Misanthropy pig-rooted out to the course, and up and down in the Parade, and round and about as the field worked up to the Barrier. And he shook his great black bony head and arched his neck and pawed till the red dust flew.

"Thoroughbred!" yelled someone in the crowd. "Itchin' for the start!"

A burst of laughter. But it was a fact that Misanthropy was one of the few horses in the field that showed the restiveness of a true-born racehorse. The rest for the most part moved about as though still back in the cattle camps from whence they came.

"Thousand to one on him!" yelled someone else.

More laughter. Then—"They're off!"

Misanthropy shot away with the rest. Thunder of hoofs and whirl of dust. Heaving mass of flapping silks and rumps and streaming manes and tails. For a moment Paddy was stupefied. Not so his horse. Misanthropy had been well trained of late in the business of starting; for Paddy had rigged up a bit of a course at Skinny Creek, with a barrier of sorts and a length of white railing and all the horses of his little station ridden by his children and the blacks to make up a field. Misanthropy had become well used to barging his way through this docile field and getting first place on the rails. He did it now, and quickly, though he started in the middle of the field. Paddy recovered his wits to find the white rail whizzing past his near-side stirrup and the field behind.

First furlong. Paddy looked under his arm. The field was crowding on his heels. The Goanna was right behind, coveting his place, waiting to slip up into it. And running neck and neck with The Goanna were Five Stars and Mailoonga, who were other well-favored horses.

Second furlong. Misanthropy still holding the lead. Oh how the watching Blisses yelled. Misanthropy! Misanthropy! Perhaps it was this uproarious demonstration of their faith that inspired the sly bookies to instill the same faith into other innocents by crying, "I'll lay fifty to one Misanthropy—Misanthropy fifty to one!"

Third furlong. Five Starts running neck and neck with Misanthropy. Mailoonga at Five Stars' girth. The Favorite still on the rails behind. Now the odds against Misanthropy were thirty to one and being taken.

Fourth furlong. Positions unaltered and the pace still steady. Odds against Misanthropy down to tens and being taken wholesale. The Blisses nearly hoarse.

Then Five Stars began to forge ahead. Soon he was leading by a length. And behind him came the Favorite, swinging from the rails, slipping up on the Wonder's flank, and up and up till Paddy could see his flaming muzzle. And Mailoonga crept up to neck and neck. Paddy used whip and spurs.

Fifth furlong. Sixth. Deafening drum of flying hoofs. Roaring of straining lungs and clatter of whips. The Straight ahead. All out—all out to win!

Misanthropy slipped away from Mailoonga, crept up on Five Stars.

"Misanthropy—Misanthropy! Gosh—look at him!"

Five to one Misanthropy. Three to one. Even money—even money! New life in the Blisses' lungs. They're ramping mad. Misanthropy will win—will win! Even money on him—odds on!

Up on Five Stars, up and up, muzzle to stirrup, muzzle to shoulder, girth to girth. And up and up—still up. "Misanthropy! Gosh who'd 'a thought it! Misanthropy! Misanthropy! Gawstrewth!"

And then—"The Favorite—the Favorite—The Goanna!"

The Favorite came up on Five Stars. Up and up he came. Muzzle to stirrup, girth to girth—"The Favorite!"

"Misanthropy—Misanthropy! No—it's the Favorite—he'll win!"

The Straight. And Misanthropy half a length ahead. The Favorite passing Five Stars. Thunder of flying hoofs. Ear-piercing din of shouting. "Misanthropy—Goanna—Misanthropy—Goanna!"

Now those two running neck and neck. Outstretched foaming neck and neck. Gain of an inch to The Goanna. Another inch. Another. Gain of a foot. The froth-flakes fly.

Matter of yards to the winning-post.

"Show 'em—show 'em—show 'em!" Paddy screamed.

Tom Hazzit knew that he would win. On that same mount he had won the Handicap twice already. He looked back at Paddy, saw the agony in his eyes, and, almost without thinking, checked his mount.

Matter of feet. Misanthropy shot ahead. Misanthropy leading by a neck.

The Post!

"Misanthropy wins—Misanthropy wins! Gosh what a race it was! Gosh look at him—look at him—he's still going —Ha! Ha! Ha!"

Misanthropy thundered on. When Paddy tried to stop him he bucked, pitched Paddy off, then flew at the off-side rails, cleared them like a bird, and disappeared in a cloud of dust toward the ranges and Skinny Creek.

The O'Dowds at Home

Patrick White

ABOUT THIS TIME Amy Parker received a message from her neighbor, Mrs. O'Dowd, by hand of a little girl called Pearl Britt, whose father worked on the road.

Mrs. O'Dowd had written on a piece of paper:

> *Tuesday morning*
>
> *Dear Mrs. Parker,*
>
> *I am in some trouble, and would take it kindly if I could see a friend.*
>
> *Your ever truly,*
>
> *(Mrs.) K. O'Dowd*

"Thank you, Pearl," said Mrs. Parker to the little girl, who continued to stand there, picking her nose and stamping her hard feet in the dust to throw the flies off her ankles. "I shall come down pretty soon."

Then Pearl ran away, pulling the head off a daisy as she went, to play a game of petals with.

When she had changed the position of one or two things and put on her hat, Amy Parker was ready to go. She caught the mare, who was swishing her tail under a willow, and got out the second-hand buggy, which by this time had grown dilapidated, while still showing signs of its decent origin. Then she would have gone in search of her husband, but stopped herself. I will not say anything, she said, in case he is angry. Now she was really ready.

All along the road that had once been theirs exclusively, people had ceased to be neighbors except in history and by sentiment. Some people nodded to Mrs. Parker as she jogged along, but others considered she was trying to find out something about them, and frowned. In fact, she was thinking of her friend and neighbor, and the lives they had lived on that road, when it ran through the unbroken scrub. But people were not to know this. Fences had made the land theirs, and they resented the intrusion of a strange face. For Mrs. Parker was by now unknown to some. She drove on through scenes she could no longer claim.

The bush had opened up. There was a man tilling the chocolate soil in between his orange trees. Outside a gray shack an old man sat beside his hollyhock. Children spilled from the doors of bursting cottages. Washing blew. It was gay on this morning, as Amy Parker had not seen it, along the two mile to O'Dowds'. Bright birds fell from the sky, and ascended. Voices could be heard where once the sound of the axe barely cut the silence, and your heart beat quicker for its company. But man had come, if it was not the Irish. Wire wound through the scrub. Many uses were found for bags and tin. And at night they sat around, the men with their shirts open on the hair of their chests, the women with their blouses easy, and drank whatever came to hand, as a comfort. If it was sometimes the kerosene, well, that too is drinkable. And more children were got to the tune of the iron beds.

The old mare that Mrs. Parker drove jogged along this rather joyful road, but her hoofs began to drag as she eased down that last stretch into the dip before O'Dowds'. The brakes were on now, so that the wheels grated on the sandstones. What is this trouble? asked Mrs. Parker, moistening her fresh lips, as she remembered it *was* a trouble had brought her that morning to O'Dowds'. And she would have prolonged her journey that seemed to plunge down.

It was a poor lot of land before you came to O'Dowds' selection, and that too was inclined to be poor, but there they had camped down, in the beginning, and got used to it. They were possessed by the land, and the land was theirs. Now all the country round about appeared quite desolate to Mrs. Parker, driving down. All trees in this part seemed to have taken desperate shapes. Some definitely writhed. Some were stuck with black hairy knobs or dismal gray cones. There was a monotonous drumming in that part of the bush, of heat and insect life. Nobody would ever want it. They threw things into it. There was a glint of old tin, and the ribs of dead animals.

So Mrs. Parker grew lower. Although a comparatively young and robust woman, of some experience, she began to feel inside her a thinness of insufficiency. She had never come close to death, and wondered whether she could deal with it. If death it was that beckoned from O'Dowds'. Though there was no reason to suppose. Instead, she began to think of her two growing children and her solid husband, and to persuade herself of her own strength. By degrees it did become plausible. Turning in through what had been the gate, her strong young shoulders swayed with the buggy and tossed off all doubts. There were moments when she was superb, and this was one. Her strong, rather thick black eyebrows glistened in the light.

So Amy Parker drove up to O'Dowds' door, and if there was no sign of death, there was little enough of life. There were two brown ducks with pointed sterns paddling and dipping in some thin mud. A red sow lay on her side and exposed her leather teats. Under the pepper tree the meat-safe hung, and swung, round and round, slowly on a wire. And the house was the same as it had always been, supporting itself on itself, and the hole in the side window still stuffed with a bag.

Amy Parker went looking for someone when she had chained the wheel, and eventually the face of her friend did come at her through a crack, and it seemed as if shortly everything must be explained.

"You will excuse me," said Mrs. O'Dowd, manipulating her moist gums, so that the words would pass, and the stubborn door, so that her friend Mrs. Parker might squeeze inside, "you must excuse me," she said, "if I sent for you in writun, my dear, makun it seem official, like, an I did think at the time, but the kiddy is forgetful that brought it, if her legs are strong. So for that reason I put pen to paper. An now you 'uv come. An I am glad."

She held a dishcloth in her hand, and that cloth was very gray, and gave out a smell of all the old dishwater it had ever been in, probably gray water too.

"Yes, I am here," said Mrs. Parker, who was feeling out of breath.

It was perhaps constricted in the kind of hugger-mugger

back kitchen, or storeroom, or dairy, or larder in which they stood, and in which it seemed most of the possessions of O'Dowds were cluttered. There were the buckets not yet washed from that morning's milking, and the bodies of several flies in that morning's milk. Several lines of old washed-out shirts and chemises—or were they rags?—hung from overhead, sawing at each other, stiff and dry, catching in the hair, in the small dark space of that room, where your ankles jostled the empty bottles that O'Dowd had not yet flung away. There was a rat trap on a deal table, baited with a lump of yellow cheese, and beside it on a big white dish a piece of dry mutton. Everything that was gathered there seemed to have been put where it could be found, and that is more than can be said for tidiness.

"It is homely, like, as you know, but what can you do?" said Mrs. O'Dowd with a sideways look as she flicked at a fly with the dishcloth and trimmed a splinter of meat from the mutton.

"Then you are well?" said Mrs. Parker her friend.

"An why should I be sick? It is not me health that has ever troubled me, Mrs. Parker. It is something far more complicayted."

She sucked the air between her gums, as if the teeth were still there, and looked at the little window that the cobwebs had almost closed up.

So Mrs. Parker waited, till her friend should give her a glimpse of something interesting, or horrible, or sad.

"It is him," she said finally. "It is that bastard. He is on it again."

"Is he ever off?" asked Mrs. Parker, who had begun to mark time.

"Not that you could notice. But there are occasions when he makes it a welter. An this is one of those. This is the biggest welter," Mrs. O'Dowd said.

"And what am I to do?" Mrs. Parker asked.

"Why, talk to him, my dear, as a woman, an a mother, an a neighbor, and an old friend. Wheedle him a bit."

"How am I to wheedle that you can't?"

Because this was something that Mrs. Parker did not care about. She was all red and spirited in the small room.

"I don't see," Mrs. Parker said.

"Ah," said Mrs. O'Dowd. "I am only his wife, an that not quite. It is different for a friend, for he will be less inclined to punch you in the face or kick you in the stomach for your pains. Just talk to him reasonable, an you so nice, he'll be cryun salt tears of remorse in a winkun, an all will be over, you will see."

"Where is he?" Mrs. Parker asked.

"He is on the back veranda, settun with his shotgun, an a bottle of eaudy Cologne, which is all we'uv got left. But the gun is only for show, Mrs. Parker, take it from me, I know his ways."

"I think it would be better," said Mrs. Parker, who did not like this a bit, "I think it would be better if we allowed the eaudy Cologne to run its course, if that's the end of the bottles, as you say. Then he will fall asleep. That is the more natural solution, it seems to me."

"Ha," laughed Mrs. O'Dowd. "No solution is natural where that bugger's concerned. He would go to town on his own breath if he was put to it. No, Mrs. Parker, it is his conscience that must be appealed to. You wouldn't forsake an old friend."

All this time the house had been quite still. You would not have thought that it contained a situation and that a difficult one. The walls of the small room were simple slab, which they had pasted over with the newspapers, and the flies had done the rest. Amy Parker had never particularly noticed before that there was print to read, but began now to pick out, in slow words, the life of a grazier who had died after an accident with a bull.

Then the feet began to stir. There was a slurring of boots over boards. O'Dowd, she remembered, had large feet.

"Hsst!" said his wife behind her hand, on which was the broad wedding ring that she wore for convenience. "That is him. He's for condescendun. Whether it's for better or worse remains to be seen. Sometimes I think it is better if he sets."

The feet had no intention but to move. They came on. They were moving over boards, some of which protested. The house was groaning. A body, that of a large man, was jostling those rooms through which it passed.

"I think we will be for movun ourselves," Mrs. O'Dowd said. "Come, dear. This way."

And Amy Parker felt the grain of her friend's hand.

"If it is a crisis he wants," said Mrs. O'Dowd, "then it is better to have a choice of avenues, as I discovered on a former occasion, an have not forgot since."

So they were whirling through the kitchen, through the smell of cold fat and ash, and were in a kind of small passage, frail certainly, but with several openings. There was a sound of listening, as loud as the silence could make it. Mrs. O'Dowd stood with the lobe of her right ear cocked on a finger.

Then he burst through a door that was obviously cardboard, as was the whole house. It flapped. O'Dowd was terrible. His mouth was moist, and the hairs were black in his nose.

"Ah," he cried. "Two!"

"Surprised I am," said his wife, "that you are not seeun more."

"Why," O'Dowd bellowed, "as if two flickun women is not enough."

And he stood there most positively, holding an ugly sort of a gun, that Amy Parker hoped would not go off.

"Mr. O'Dowd," she said, "don't you recognize me?"

"Yes," said his wife, "it is our old friend Mrs. Parker. Come to pay us a visit for old times' sake."

"My arse," said O'Dowd. "A couple o' flickun women, an you have a funeral."

"That is a nice way to speak to a lady," protested Mrs. O'Dowd.

"I am not nice," said her husband simply.

His eyes frowned on this truth as if he could not look at it too long or too closely. It was a pretty pebble of a thing that required much examination.

Then he took his gun and shot it off.

"God help us!" shrieked his wife, holding her hair, that was coming down in bundles about her ears. "That we have come to this in our own home, Christians notwithstandun."

"Are you hit?" asked Amy Parker, who had felt the wind.

"I can't answer for every part of me body," Mrs. O'Dowd cried. "It's the fright I got. You black bugger! You devul! You'll kill us yet!"

"What else do you think I am flickun well aimun at? Damn woman!"

And he took the gun again.

"Quick," said Mrs. O'Dowd. "Mrs. Parker, we must make tracks!"

And in that small space of brown passage, with the flinty smell of the gun and its hot oil, there was such a flapping of women, revolving, and beating against the walls, as they chose some opening through which to escape. In this scrimmage Amy Parker became separated from her friend and found herself in the best room, with the bit of a door to shut and hope against. Where her friend went to she did not know, only she had removed herself in that same gyration of anxiety and skirt.

"Flick me if it ain't finished," O'Dowd had begun to bellow.

He could have been breaking his gun the other side of the door, and there was such a slapping of his pockets, as if he were on fire.

"Sold out," he roared. "But I will get her," he said, "if I wring her balley neck."

After a door had crashed, and the house had shaken and settled again, they seemed to have entered a fresh phase, of peace, or inverted frenzy. In the room in which Amy Parker stood, which was the best at O'Dowd's, and for that reason never used, even the soul suspected it would never rise. Roses had been pasted in wrinkles over every possible crack of escape, with the result that life had given up and was littering the window sill with wings and shells and pale spidery legs. The intruder, already petrified, was received into the presence of the greater mummies, the sofa, with hair sprouting from the shoulders, and on the mantelpiece a long cat, that O'Dowd had stuffed for his wife, who had been fond of it.

Turning with an effort from the sad cat, Amy Parker looked through the fog of the window and saw her neighbor elongate herself catwise round the corner of a shed, the ears appearing to be flattened back, and in her glassy eyes the desperate hope of self-protection. Then the observer would have told her friend that she need no longer fear the gun but she could not tear the window open, and as the sound of knuckles on the glass was terrible in the deathly room, all attempts to attract attention were fizzling fatefully out. So Mrs. O'Dowd continued to crane and flatten, as if she were expecting death to appear from some direction she could not think of, much as she racked her brains.

As Amy Parker was struggling to break the terrible bonds of her protective room, O'Dowd came round the corner of the house, carrying the cleaver as if it were a little flag.

Then it is true, Mrs. Parker could not scream against the glass.

She saw the gristle come in Mrs. O'Dowd's throat as she flattened herself still flatter against the shed. Before she ran, round the corner of the house. And O'Dowd running, carrying his little flag.

Then Amy Parker was freed. She burst out, she ran, not because she was brave, but because the thread of her life had become attached to the same spool that was winding O'Dowds round the house. So Amy Parker ran too, down the rickety step, against the fuchsia tree, that tingled as she passed. She ran, in turn, round the house, which had become the only pivot of existence; without it they were lost.

They were running and running, though sometimes also lurching, whether it was from the grog, or the slippery pineneedles on that side, or the stones and the potholes on the other, or just because somebody's corns gave a twinge that was extra bad. But running. That was the desperate thing. And bits of the house flashed past, through windows and doors, the boxes in which they had led their stale lives —why, there was the loaf lying that the woman had cut crooked that morning, and the pair of pants the man had let fall from his thighs, and let lie, in black coils. Such glimpses flittered. And the flattened cat on her varnished stand on the mantelpiece. She had been called Tib, Amy Parker remembered, from behind her breath.

Where are we going to? she asked. At the moment death seemed terrible hard to catch. The back of O'Dowd fluctuated. At times she wondered what she would do if she could run fast enough. But the back of O'Dowd lurched round the next corner. Always.

There were moments when, through the straining air, she swore that she heard the man hack off his wife's head with the chopper. She knew the thud, and had seen before, somewhere, the white pipe gasping words of forgiveness in the dust. We will have to do something with the body, she said, before the constable comes.

But in the meantime she was running, in the same cloud that several fowls had formed, as if disturbed by the prospect of chopping. The fowls' long skinny necks were stretched right out. They were extended in general motion. And a pig too. The same red sow raced in the race, her teats hitting her ribs, grunting and farting as she galloped, with every sign of mirth, or perhaps terror, it was difficult to tell. The fowls shot off at a tangent, but the sow continued, out of dedication to man.

Round and round man ran, till he had come on quite a distance into that country in which he is prepared to suffer, sometimes rolling his eyeballs, sometimes giving, in the depths of his fixed eyes, melancholy glimpses of the static world of peace that he has lost. In this way Amy Parker, when she had all but bust, saw her husband and her two children, seated at the kitchen table, drinking tea out of white cups, the crumbs of Tuesday's cake falling yellow from the corners of their mouths. And she could have cried. She did, in fact, just begin to blubber, for herself, no longer for her friend.

"Mrs. Parker," Mrs. O'Dowd was panting just then.

So that Mrs. Parker, looking round, saw that Mrs. O'Dowd, by exerting herself tremendously, had managed to catch up. The gray blur of her face was mostly mouth and eyes.

"What are we to do now?" Mrs. Parker panted in return.

For they were still running and running round the house, somewhere ahead, or else at the tail of O'Dowd.

"Pray to God," Mrs. O'Dowd hissed.

And the two women did, after a fashion, resuming an acquaintance they had not kept up, even hinting they had been neglected. They ran and prayed.

Then at the corner by the big tank it happened quite suddenly that they met O'Dowd, who had had the brilliant notion of running in the opposite direction. He was wet, and black, with the chopper in his hand.

"Ahhh!" cried his wife. "It is you at last. I am ready for whatever it is you intend to do. It is not me that ever denied you nothun. Here I am."

She stood still, in the last fragments of herself and her

tormented hair. Out of her bosom, on to her blouse, had bumped the holy medals that she wore for safety.

"So help me God," she said, "I was not bad, an I was not good, so chop quick, an let us have the judgment."

Then O'Dowd, who was bigger than ever, and the drink lighting him up with intemperate fire, began to tremble, and his flag flapped, the little chopper that he carried in his hand.

"Ah," he cried, "it is the devul that got inter me. An the eudy Cologne."

Till he was crying and protesting, and his lips, that had been thinned out by sun and running, were full again.

"It is me nature, I am like this," he cried. "I am up an down. It *isn't* that there is actual bad in me, if there is not actual good. I am a middlun man. It is only when the drink takes hold that I get a bit above meself, and then would do no harm, onyway, I am pretty certain not."

"Then we know now," said his wife, who had sat down where she was, in a few tufts of yellow grass and dead leaves and dust. "Then it is all cleared up quite convenient, an we are more alive than dead. That is the main thing. It is obligun of you, my dear, to explain the situation."

"Yes," he said, wiping his nose, that was getting out of hand, "it is all over now. An I will take a little nap, Mrs. Parker, if you don't mind. It will be good for me. Just now I am not meself."

Mrs. O'Dowd sat shredding grass, and her friend, who was above her, had become a monument. As O'Dowd began to move his body with some care across the yard, stepping so as to avoid the dead emotions, and carrying his little implement as if it were a piece of paper, that he would roll up, now that it was no more use, and put away. Then he went into the house, after bashing his forehead on the lintel, and crying out because he did not deserve it.

Mrs. O'Dowd began to hum. She shredded grass. She was making a comb-and-paper noise. And her hair was hanging down.

"Will you leave him?" Mrs. Parker asked.

But O'Dowd hummed.

"I would not stand for any such nonsense, not from any man, not from a husband," said Mrs. Parker, shifting her stone limbs.

"But I like him," said Mrs. O'Dowd, throwing aside the dead grass. "We are suited to each other," she said.

And she began to manipulate her legs, that were under her, and that had begun to set into a permanent shape from being poured there molten.

"Aoh," she said. "I could'uv killed him, notwithstandun, if it had been *my* hand had held the little axe, an us runnun round the house for fun."

Now Amy Parker had gone to release the wheel of the buggy in the shafts of which the old horse stood looking, and her friend had turned and gone back into the house, putting up her hair through the long trance that life can become.

"Oh, an Mrs. Parker," she said, putting her head out through a window, "I had forgot. Would you like a nice piece of cheese, that was made by me own hand? It is mature an nice."

But Amy Parker shook her head, and the old horse pulled. They were going. Through a trance of trees and all that had not happened.

Pear Tree Dance

Elizabeth Jolley

NO ONE KNEW where the Newspaper of Claremont Street went in her spare time.

Newspaper or Weekly as she was called by those who knew her, earned her living by cleaning other people's houses. There was something she wanted to do more than anything else, and for this she needed money. For a long time she had been saving, putting money aside in little amounts. Every morning, when she woke up, she thought about her money. The growing sum danced before her, growing a little more. She calculated what she would be able to put in the bank. She was not very quick at arithmetic. As she lay in bed she used the sky as a blackboard, and in her mind, wrote the figures on the clouds. The total sum came out somewhere half way down her window.

While she was working in the different houses she sang, *"the bells of hell go ting a ling a ling for you and not for me."* She liked hymns best.

"Well 'ow are we?" she called out when she went in in the mornings. "Ow's everybody today?" And she would throw open windows and start pulling the stove to pieces. She knew everything about all the people she cleaned for and she never missed anything that was going on.

"I think that word should be clay—C.L.A.Y." She helped old Mr. Kingston with his crossword puzzle.

"Chattam's girl's engaged at long larst," she reported to the Kingstons. "Two rooms full of presents, yo' should just see!"

"Kingston's boy's 'ad 'orrible accident." she described the details to the Chathams. "Lorst 'is job first, pore boy! Pore Mrs. Kingston!" Weekly sadly shook the table cloth over the floor and carried out some dead roses carefully as if to keep them for the next funeral.

"I could not do without Thee Thou Saviour of the Lorst," she sang at the Butterworths.

She cleaned in all sorts of houses. Her body was hard like a board and withered with so much work she seemed to have stopped looking like a woman.

On her way home from work she always went in the little shop at the end of Claremont Street and bought a few things, taking her time and seeing who was there and watching what they bought.

"Here's the Newspaper of Claremont Street," the two shop girls nudged each other.

"Any pigs been eating babies lately Newspaper?" one of them called out.

"What happened to the man who sawed off all his fingers at the timber mill?" the other girl called. "You never finished telling us."

No one needed to read anything; the Newspaper of Claremont Street told them all the news.

One Tuesday afternoon when she had finished her work, she went to look at the valley for the first time. All the morning she was thinking about the long drive. She wondered which would be the shortest way to get to this place hidden behind the pastures and foothills along the South West Highway. It was a strain thinking about it and talking gossip at the same time, especially as she kept thinking, too, that she had no right really to go looking at land.

All land is somebody's land. For Weekly the thought of possessing some seemed more of an impertinence than a possibility. Perhaps this was because she had spent her childhood in a slaty backyard where nothing would grow except thin carrots and a few sunflowers. All round the place where she lived the slag heaps smouldered and hot cinders fell on the paths. The children gathered to play in a little thicket of stunted thornbushes and elderberry trees. There were patches of coltsfoot and they picked the yellow flowers eagerly till none was left. Back home in the Black Country where it was all coal mines and brick kilns and iron foundries her family had never had a house or a garden. Weekly had nothing behind her, not even the place where she was born. It no longer existed. As soon as she was old enough she was sent into service. Later she left her country with the family where she was employed. All her life she had done domestic work. She was neat and quick and clean and her hands were rough like nutmeg graters and she knew all there was to know about people and their ways of living.

Weekly lived in a rented room; it was covered with brown linoleum, which she polished. The house was built a long time ago for a large family but now the house was all divided up. Every room had a different life in it and every life was isolated from all the other lives.

Except for the old car she bought, Weekly, the Newspaper of Claremont Street, had no possessions. Nothing in the room belonged to her except some old books and papers, collected and hoarded, and her few washed-out and mended clothes. She lived quite alone and, when she came home tired after her long day of work, she took some bread and boiled vegetables from the fly-screen cupboard where she kept her food, and she sat reading and eating hungrily. She was so thin and her neck so scraggy that when she swallowed you could see the food going down. But as she had no one there to see and to tell her about it, it did not really matter. While it was still light, Weekly pulled her chair across to the narrow window of her room and sat bent over her mending. She darned everything. She put on patches with a herringbone stitch. Sometimes she made the worn out materials of her skirts firmer with rows of her-ring-boning, one row neatly above the other, the brown thread glowing in those last rays of the sun that make all browns beautiful. Even the old linoleum could have a sudden richness at this time of the evening. It was like the quick lighting up of a plain girl's face when she smiles because of some unexpected happiness.

It was when she was driving out to the country on Sundays in her old car she began to wish for some land, nothing very big, just a few acres. She drove about and stared into green paddocks fenced with round poles for horses and scattered in the corners with red flame-tree flowers and splashed all over with white lilies. She stopped to admire almond blossom and she wished for a little weatherboard house, warm in the sun, fragrant with orange trees and surrounded by vines. Sometimes she sat for hours alone in the scrub of a partly cleared piece of bush and stared at the few remaining tall trees, wondering at their age, and at the yellow tufts of Prickly Moses surviving.

The advertisements describing land for sale made her so excited she could hardly read them. As soon as she read one she became so restless she wanted to go off at once to have a look.

"Yo' should 'ave seen the mess after the Venns' Party," she called to Mrs. Lacy. "Broken glass everywhere, blood on the stairs, and a whole pile of half-eaten pizzas in the laundry. Some people think they're having a good time! And you'll never believe this, I picked up a bed jacket, ever so pretty it was, to wash it and, would you believe, there was a yuman arm in it . . ." The Newspaper of Claremont Street talked all the time in the places where she worked. It was not for nothing she was called Newspaper or Weekly, but all the time she was talking she never spoke about the land. Secretly she read her advertisements and secretly she went off to look.

She first went to the valley on a Tuesday after work.

"Tell about Sophie Whiteman," Diana Lacey tried to detain Weekly. Mrs. Lacey had, as usual, gone to town and Diana was in bed with a sore throat.

"Wash the curtains please," Mrs. Lacey felt this was a precaution against more illness. "We must get rid of the nasty germs," she said. "And Weekly, I think the dining-room curtains need a bit of sewing, if you have time, thank you," and she had rushed off late for the hairdresser.

"Well," said Weekly putting away the ironing board. "She got a pair of scissors and she went into the garding and she looked all about her to see no one was watching and she cut up a earthworm into a whole lot of little pieces."

"What did her mother do?" asked Diana joyfully, knowing from a previous telling.

"Well," said Weekly, "she come in from town and took orf her hat and her lovely fur coat, very beautiful lady, Mrs. Whiteman, she took orf her good clothes and she took Sophie Whiteman and laid her acrorss her lap and give her a good hidin'."

"Oh!" Diana was pleased. "Was that before she died of the chocolate lining in her stomach or after?"

"Diana Lacey, what have I told you before, remember? Sophie Whiteman had her good hidin' afore she died. How could she cut up a worm after she died. Use yor brains!"

Weekly was impatient to leave to find the way to the valley. She found a piece of paper and scrawled a note for Mrs. Lacey.

Will come early tomorrow to run up yor curtings W.

She knew she had to cross the Medulla brook and turn left at the twenty-nine-mile peg. She found the valley all right.

After the turn off, the road bends and climbs and then there it is, pasture on either side of the road with cattle grazing, straying toward a three-cornered dam. And, on that first day, there was a newly born calf that seemed unable to get up.

She saw the weatherboard house and she went up there and knocked.

"Excuse me, but can yo' tell me what part of the land's for sale?" her voice trembled.

The young woman, the tenant's wife, came out.

"It's all for sale," she said. They walked side by side.

"All up there," the young woman pointed to the hillside where it was steep and covered with dead trees and rocks and pig sties made from old railway sleepers and corrugated iron. Beyond was the light and shade of the sun shining through the jarrah trees.

"And down there," she flung her plump arm toward the meadow that lay smiling below.

"There's a few orange trees, neglected," she explained. "That in the middle is an apricot. That over there is a pear tree. And where you see them white lilies, that's where there's an old well. Seven acres this side."

They walked back toward the house.

"The pasture's leased just now," the young woman said. "But it's all for sale too, thirty acres and there's another eighteen in the scrub."

Weekly wanted to stay looking at the valley but she was afraid that the young woman would not believe she really wanted to buy some of it. She drove home in a golden tranquility dreaming of her land embroidered with pear blossom and bulging with plump apricots. Her crooked feet were wet from the long weeds and yellow daisies of the damp meadows The road turned and dropped. Below was the great plain. The neat ribs of the vineyards chased each other toward the vague outlines of the city. Beyond was a thin line shining like the rim of a china saucer. It was the sea, brimming, joining the earth to the sky.

While she scrubbed and cleaned she thought about the land and what she would grow there. At night she studied pamphlets on fruit growing. She had enough money saved to buy a piece of land but she still felt she had no right.

Every Sunday she went out to look at the valley and every time she found something fresh. Once she noticed that on one side of the road was a whole long hedge of white wild roses. Another time it seemed as if sheep were on the hillside among the pig sties, but, when she climbed up, she saw it was only the light on some grayish bushes making them look like a quiet flock of sheep.

One evening she sat in the shop in Claremont Street, sucking in her cheeks and peering into other people's shopping bags.

"Last week yo' bought flour," she said to a woman.

"So what if I did?"

"Well you'll not be needing any terday," Weekly advised. "Now eggs yo' didn't get, yo'll be needing them! . . ."

"Pore Mr. Kingston," Weekly shook her head and addressed the shop "I done 'is puzzle today. 'Mr. Kingston,' I said, 'let me do your crossword'—I doubt he'll leave his bed again." Silence fell among the groceries and the women who were shopping. The silence remained unbroken for Weekly had forgotten to talk. She had slipped into thinking about the valley. All her savings were not enough, not even for a part of the meadows. She was trying to get over the terrible disappointment she had just had.

"If you're prepared to go out say forty miles," Mr. Rusk, the land agent, had said gently, "there's a nice five acres with a tin shack for tools. Some of it's river flats, suitable for pears. That would be within your price range." Mr. Rusk spoke seriously to the old woman even though he was not sure whether she was all right in the head. "Think it over," he advised. He always regarded a customer as a buyer until the customer did not buy.

Weekly tried to forget the valley, she began to scatter the new land with pear blossom. She would go at the weekend.

"Good night all!" She left the shop abruptly without telling any news at all.

On Sunday Weekly went to look at the five acres. It was more lovely than she had expected, and fragrant. A great many tall trees had been left standing and the tin shack turned out to be a tiny weatherboard cottage. She was afraid she had come to the wrong place.

"It must be someone's home." she thought to herself as she peered timidly through the cottage window and saw that it was full of furniture. Disappointment crept over her. Purple pig face was growing everywhere and, from the high verandah, she looked across the narrow valley to a hay field between big trees. There was such a stillness that Weekly felt more than ever that she was trespassing, not only on the land, but into the very depths of the stillness itself.

Mr. Rusk said that it was the five acres he had meant.

"I've never been there myself," he explained when she told him about the cottage. "Everything's included in the price."

Buying land takes time but Weekly contained herself in silence and patience, working hard all the days.

She began to buy things, a spade, rubber boots, some candles and groceries and polish and she packed them into the old car. Last of all she bought a pear tree, it looked so wizened she wondered how it could ever grow. Carefully she wrapped it in wet newspapers and laid it like a thin baby along the back seat.

On the day Mr. Rusk gave her the key, Weekly went to work with it pinned inside her dress. She felt it against her ribs all morning and in the afternoon she drove out to her piece of land.

The same trees and fragrance and the cottage were all there as before. This time she noticed honeysuckle and roses, a fig tree, and a hedge of rosemary all neglected now and waiting for her to continue what some other person had started many years ago.

She thought she would die there that first day as she opened the cottage door to look inside. She looked shyly at the tiny rooms and wandered about on the land looking at it and breathing the warm fragrance. The noise of the magpies poured into the stillness and she could hear the creek, in flood, running. She sank down on to the earth as if she would never get up from it again. She counted over the treasures of the cottage. After having nothing she seemed now to have everything, a bed, table, chairs and in the kitchen, a wood stove and two toasting forks, a kettle, and five flat irons. There was a painted cupboard too and someone had made curtains of pale-blue stuff patterned with roses.

Weekly wanted to clean out the cottage at once. She felt suddenly too tired. She rested on the earth and looked about her feeling the earth with her hands and listening as if she expected some great wisdom to come to her from the quiet trees and the undergrowth of the bush.

At about five o'clock the sun, before falling into the scrub, flooded the slope from the west and reddened the white bark of the trees. The sky deepened with the coming evening. Weekly forced her crooked old feet into the new rubber boots. She took the spade and the thin pear tree and went down to the mud flats at the bottom of her land.

Choosing a place for the pear tree she dug a hole. It was harder to dig in the clay than she had thought it would be and she had to pause to rest several times.

She carried some dark earth from under a fallen tree over to the hole. Carefully she held the little tree in position and scattered the dark soft earth round the roots. She shook the little tree and scattered in more earth and then she firmed the soil, treading gently round and round the tree.

For the first time in her life the Newspaper of Claremont Street, or Weekly as she was called, was dancing. Stepping round and round the little tree she imagined herself to be like a bride dancing with lacy white blossom cascading on all sides. Round and round the tree, dancing, firming the softly yielding earth with her new boots. And from the little foil label blowing in the restlessness of the evening came a fragile music for the pear tree dance.

You Gave Me Hyacinths

Janette Turner Hospital

SUMMER COMES HOT and steamy with the heavy smell of raw sugar to the northeast coast of Australia. The cane pushes through the rotting window blinds and grows into the cracks and corners of the mind. It ripens in the heart at night, and its crushed sweetness drips into dreams. I have woken brushing from my eyelids the silky plumes that burst up into harvest time. And I have stood smoke-blackened as the cane fires licked the night sky, and kicked my way through the charred stubble after the men have slashed at the naked stalks and sent them churning through the mill. I have walked forever through the honeyed morning air to the crumbling high school—brave outpost of another civilization.

The class always seemed to be on the point of bulging out the windows. If I shut my eyes and thought hard I could probably remember all the faces and put a name to each. One never forgets that first year out of teachers' college, the first school, the first students. Dellis comes before anyone else, of course, feline and demanding, blotting out the others; Dellis, who sat stonily bored through classes and never turned in homework and wrote nothing at all on test papers. "Can't understand poetry," she said by way of explanation. There were detentions and earnest talks. At least, I was earnest; Dellis was bored. She put her case simply: "I'll fail everything anyway."

"But you don't *need* to, Dellis. It's a matter of your attitude, not your ability. What sort of job will you get if you don't finish high school?"

"Valesi's store. Or the kitchen at the mill canteen."

"Yes, well. But they will be very monotonous jobs, don't you think? Very boring."

"Yes." Flicking back the long blonde hair.

"Now just supposing you finished high school. Then what would you do?"

"Same thing. Work at Valesi's or in the mill canteen. Till I'm married. Everybody does."

"You could go to Brisbane, or even Sydney or Melbourne. There are any number of jobs you could get there if you were to finish high school. There would be theaters to go to, plays to see. And libraries. Dellis, this town doesn't even have a library."

Silence.

"Have you ever been out of this town, Dellis?"

"Been to Cairns once."

Cairns. Twenty thousand people, and less than a hundred miles away: the local idea of the Big City.

"Dellis, what are you going to do with your life?"

No answer.

I felt angry, as though I were the one trapped in the slow rhythm of a small tropical town. "Can you possibly be content," I asked viciously, "to work at the mill, get married, have babies, and grow old in this shriveled-up sun-blasted village?"

She was mildly puzzled at my outburst, but shrugged it off as being beyond her. "Reckon I'll have to marry the first boy who knocks me up," she said.

"You don't *have* to marry anybody, Dellis. No doubt you could fall in love with some boy in this town and be quite happy with him. But is that all you want?"

"Dunno. It's better'n *not* getting married."

I knew her parents were not around; perhaps they were dead; though more likely they were merely deserters who had found the lure of fruit picking in the south too rewarding to resist. I knew she lived with a married sister—the usual shabby wooden cottage with toddlers messily underfoot, everyone cowering away from the belligerent drunk who came home from the cane fields each night. The family, the town—it was an intolerable cocoon. She simply had to fight her way out of it, go south. I told her so. But her face was blank. The world beyond the town held neither fascination nor terror. I think she doubted the existence of anything beyond Cairns.

In the classroom the air was still and fetid. There was the stale sweat of forty students; there was also the sickly odor of molasses rolling in from the mill. An insistent wave of nausea lapped at me. Dellis's face seemed huge and close and glistened wetly the way all flesh did in the summer. She looked bored as always, though probably not so much at her detention as at the whole wearying business of an afternoon and evening still to be lived through—after which coolness would come for an hour or two, and even fitful sleep. Then another dank day would begin.

"Dellis, let's get out of here. Will you go for a walk with me?"

"Okay," she shrugged.

Outside the room things were immediately better. By itself, the molasses in the air was heavy and drowsy, but pleasant. We crunched down the drive and out the gate under the shade of the flame trees.

"I love those," Dellis said, pointing upward where the startling crimson flaunted itself against the sky.

"Why?"

She was suddenly angry. "Why? You always want to know why. You spoil things. I hate your classes. I hate poetry. It's stupid. Just sometimes there is a bit I like, but all you ever do is ask why. Why do I like it? And then I feel stupid because I never know why. I just like it, that's all. And you always spoil it."

We walked in silence the length of the street, which was the length of the town, past the post office, Cavallero's general store, Valesi's Snack Bar, and two pubs. The wind must have been blowing our way from the mill, because the soot settled on us gently as we walked. The men swilling their beer on the benches outside the pubs fell silent as we passed and their eyes felt uncomfortable on my damp skin. At the corner pub, someone called out "Hey, Dellis!" from the dark inside, and laughter fell into the dust as we rounded the corner and turned toward the mill.

Halfway between the corner and the mill, Dellis said suddenly, "I like the red. I had a red dress for the school dance, and naturally you know what they all said. . . . But the trees don't care. That's what I'd like to be. A flame tree." We went on in silence again, having fallen into the mesmeric pattern of stepping from sleeper to sleeper of the narrow rail siding, until we came to the line of cane cars waiting outside the mill. Dellis reached into one and pulled out two short pieces. She handed one to me and started chewing the other.

"We really shouldn't, Dellis. It's stealing."

She eyed me sideways and shrugged. "You spoil things."

I tore off strips of bamboolike skin with my teeth and sucked at the soft sweet fibers.

We had passed the mill, and were on the beach road. Two miles under that spiteful sun. Close to the cane there was some coolness, and we walked in the dusty three-foot strip between the road and the sugar plumes, sucking and chewing and spitting out the fibers. The dust came up in little puffs around our sandals. We said nothing, just chewed and spat. Only two cars passed us. The Howes all hung out of one and waved. The other was a pickup truck headed for the mill.

About one and a half miles along, the narrow road suddenly emerged from its canyon of tall cane. A lot of cutting had been done, and a farmhouse stood alone in the shorn fields, white and blinding in the afternoon sun. The haze of color around the front door was a profusion of Cooktown orchids, fragile waxen flowers, soft purple with a darker slash of purple at the heart. "Gian's house," said Dellis as we walked on, and into the cool cover of uncut cane again.

Gian! So that was why he always had an orchid to tuck brazenly behind one ear. He was seventeen years old, a Torres Strait Islander: black, six feet tall, a purple flower nestled against his curly hair any time one saw him except in class. Gian, rakishly Polynesian, bending over that day after school till the impudent orchid and his incredible eyes were level with mine.

"Did you know that I killed my father, Miss?"

"Yes, Gian. I was told that when I first arrived."

"Well?" The eyes were incongruously blue, and watchful under the long silky lashes.

I knew the court verdict was self-defense, I knew his father had been blind drunk, a wife-beater on the rampage.

"Well?" Gian persisted.

I said lamely: "It must have been horrible."

"I hated him," Gian said without passion. "He was a bastard."

"I gather many people thought so."

"Well?"

"What are you asking me, Gian? How can I know what was the right thing to do? Only you can know that."

"I am the only person in this town who has killed a man. Do you realize that?"

We stared at each other, and then outrageously he let his eyes wander slowly down my body with blatant intent, and walked away. I was trembling. After that I was always afraid to look Gian in the eye, and he always dared me to. When I turned to write on the board, I could feel two burning spots on the back of my neck. And when I faced the class again, his eyes were waiting, and a slow grin would spread across his face. Yet it was not an insolent grin. That was what was most disturbing. It seemed to say that we two shared a daring and intimate secret. But he knew it and I didn't.

Dellis and I had reached the beach. It was deserted. We kicked off our sandals, lay down, and curled our toes into the warm sand. The palms cast a spindly shade that wasn't much help, but a tired wisp of sea breeze scuffled up the sand refreshingly from the calm water. So amazingly calm inside the reef. I never could get used to it. I had grown up with frenetic surf beaches, but from here you had to go a thousand miles down the coast before you got south of the Great Reef.

"Dellis, you must visit Brisbane this summer, and give yourself a swim in the surf for a Christmas present. You just can't imagine how exciting it is."

"Let's go swimming now. It's so bloody hot."

"But we don't have swimsuits."

"Just take our clothes off."

"But somebody might come."

Dellis stood up and unbuttoned her blouse. "You spoil things," she said. It hurt when she stood naked in front of me. She was only fifteen, and it wasn't fair. I almost told her how beautiful she was, but envy and embarrassment stopped me. This is her world, I thought; she is part of it, she belongs. She was tanned all over; there were no white parts. She ran down into the water without looking back.

I stood up and slipped off my dress, but then my heart failed me, and I went into the water with my underwear on. We must have swum for half an hour, and it was cool and pleasant. Then we ran along the water's edge for ten minutes or so to dry out. We dressed and lay on the sand again. "It's good to do that," Dellis murmured. "It's the best thing when you're unhappy."

"Are you often unhappy?"

The look she gave me suggested that if I had to ask such stupid questions, why did I call myself a teacher?

"What I meant, Dellis, is that I'd like to . . . if you're unhappy, I would like to . . . I mean, if there's any way I can help. . . ."

"You don't even know how to chew cane properly." She

was looking at me with a kind of affectionate contempt, as though I were an idiot child. "You don't know anything. You really don't know *anything*." She shook her head and grinned at me.

I smiled back. I wanted to tell her how much I was learning. I would have liked to speak of poetic symbols, and of the significance that flame trees or Cooktown orchids would henceforth have for me. Instead I said: "Dellis, today. . . . Who would have thought? How could I have guessed, this morning, that today would be so . . . would be such a . . . ? Well, a *remarkable* day."

"Really? Why?"

"You spoil things. Don't ask me why."

She giggled. "But really, why?"

"It's very complicated. It has a lot to do with a religious and sheltered background that you couldn't even begin to imagine, and it would take a lot of explaining. But to put it briefly, it is a truly extraordinary thing for me to have gone swimming naked with one of my students."

"You didn't even take all your clothes off," she laughed.

Now the silence was close and comfortable, and longer and drowsier. We must have dozed, because when I sat up again the humidity was even more oppressive and monstrous dark clouds had billowed up out of the sea.

"There's going to be a thunderstorm, Dellis. We'd better get home quickly."

"Too early in the year," she said sleepily. And when she saw the clouds, "It'll ruin a lot of cane."

We were walking quickly, and nearly at Gian's house again, when Dellis pointed into the shadowy green maze of the cane field and said, "That's where Gian and I did it."

"Did what?"

"*Did* it. He laid me."

"Oh! . . . I . . . I see. Your first . . . ?"

She looked at me, startled, and laughed. "He's the only one I loved. And the only one I wouldn't take money from."

Virgin and child in a field of green. No madonna could have beheld the amazing fruit of her womb with more awed astonishment than I felt. Something hurt at the back of my head, and I reached up vaguely with my hand. There was a whole ordered moral world there somewhere. But I couldn't find it. It wouldn't come.

I said, inanely: "So you and Gian are in love?"

"He was going to give me money and I wouldn't take it. But he was gentle. And afterward he took the orchid from behind his ear and put it between my legs. I hoped I'd have a baby, but I didn't."

The storm was coming and we fled before the wind and the rain. At the mill we separated, but Dellis ran back and grabbed my arm. She had to shout, and even then I thought I hadn't heard her properly. Our skirts bucked about our legs like wet sails, runnels of water sluiced over our ears. She shouted again: "Have you ever been laid?"

"Dellis!"

"Have you?"

"This is not . . . this is not a proper. . . ."

"Have you?"

"No."

"Gian says you're beautiful. Gian says that you. . . . He says he would like to. . . . That's why I hated you. But now I don't."

Then we ran for our lives.

All through my dinner and all through the evening, the rain drummed on the iron roof, and the wind dashed the banana palms against the window in a violent tattoo. For some reason I wanted to dance to the night's jazz rhythm. But then surely there was something more insistent than the thunder, a battering on my door. She was standing dripping wet on my doorstep.

"Dellis, for God's sake, what are you doing here? It's almost midnight."

"They were fighting at home again, and I couldn't stand it. I brought something for you."

She held out a very perfect Cooktown orchid. Somebody's prize bloom, stolen.

"Come inside, out of the rain," I said vaguely, listening to the lines from Eliot that fluted in my head—fragments and images half-remembered. I had to take down the book, so I showed her the passage:

> "You gave me hyacinths first a year ago,
> "They called me the hyacinth girl."
> —Yet when we came back, late, from the
>   Hyacinth garden,
> Your arms full, and your hair wet, I could not
> Speak, and my eyes failed, I was neither
> Living nor dead, and I knew nothing,
> Looking into the heart of light, the silence.

"Dellis," I said, as (teacherly, motherly) I combed out her wet tangled hair, "for me, you will always be the hyacinth girl."

"*Poetry!*" she sniffed. And then: "What do hyacinths look like?"

"I don't know. I imagine they look like Cooktown orchids."

Thomas Awkner Floats
Tim Winton

I

ALTHOUGH HE HAD NEVER been in an airplane before, Thomas Awkner was not a complete stranger to flight. His earliest memory was of the day the swing on the back veranda propelled him across the yard and into the fence. The ground rushed beneath him. Borer holes in the wooden paling became mineshafts. Impact was devastating. A loose picket pinched his earlobe and held him captive and screaming until his father could be hounded away from his incinerator behind the shed. Now, as the big jet staggered through the turbulence out over the desert, he twisted that earlobe between his fingers and sweated. He did not like to fly. His own height gave him vertigo.

Flight attendants lurched up the aisles. Drinks spilled. The FASTEN SEATBELTS sign chimed on and off. The thirty seats ahead of him were occupied by what seemed to be a delegation from the Deaf Society. These men and women wore blazers and little berets, and for most of the flight they had been engaged in an informal celebration, creating a disconcertingly visual babble. Words ruffled up by the handful and faces stretched with laughter, impatience, urgency. All Thomas Awkner could hear was the chink of glasses, but for the Deaf Society, he decided, it must have been a rowdy affair. Watching them gave him a thirst. He pushed the button for a flight attendant.

While he waited, he swabbed the sweat from his palms and smiled at the men on either side of him. It was a desperate grin, starched with fear, but it went unnoticed. From up ahead came a sharp, solitary belch. None of the partyers in the aisle seemed embarrassed for a moment.

A flight attendant came, but fear had knotted Awkner's throat so that he found it difficult to speak. The woman raised her sculptured eyebrows at him. Awkner's lips moved, but his voice seemed to be parked somewhere back down in his throat.

"Are you well?" the fat man next to him asked.

"The poor man is deaf, sir," the flight attendant said. She began to mime eating and drinking. Thomas Awkner flinched.

The fat man scowled. "I don't think he is. He's not wearing a blazer, or even a beret."

"For God's sake, man," the triangular man on Awkner's right protested, "a man doesn't need a blazer and a beret to be deaf and dumb. He's probably freelance."

"Rubbish," the fat man said, "he's listening to us now."

"They lip read, sir," said the flight attendant.

"Could I have a beer, please?" Thomas Awkner managed to say at last.

"See? He talks."

"So what?"

"Sir, honestly, it doesn't mean a thing!"

"Emu Bitter, if I could."

The flight attendant beamed at him and went to get the drink. Neither man spoke to him. He felt as though he had upset them terribly. He wedged himself between their anger and their outsized bodies, and thought about his two hours in Melbourne. Right across the continent, he mused, long enough to deliver a manila envelope and board another plane home.

Since he was five years old, Thomas Awkner had been running family errands, taking small boxes to strange doors, relaying single words through holes in fibro walls, passing notes to men in gray hats in windy harborside streets. The Awkners took for granted his apparent idiocy and he did nothing, as he grew older, to unsettle their assumption for fear of losing his only measure of importance in the Awkner web. An idiot, they thought, was the best courier possible. Understanding could be a risk. So the young Thomas Awkner cultivated complete incuriosity; he ignored message or parcel and concentrated on the trip, feasting on the world outside the asbestos house with its smoke and secret talk. But the trip always ended with a return home where nothing more was expected of him. At home, therefore, he did nothing.

He was flying. His father had never flown: that fact made him feel sophisticated. His father was a memory associated with the endlessly smoldering incinerator behind the back shed. Boxes of shredded paper were often brought through the house at every hour of the night. He recalled that long, gray face with its seedy moustache and perennial white stubble. His father died ten years before. An aerosol can had exploded as he peered into the incinerator. Uncle Dubbo appeared out of nowhere to attend the cremation service.

His beer arrived. He drank it quickly and immediately his bladder demanded relief. Lurching down the aisle toward the rear of the plane, he felt as though he was swinging across a ravine on a rope bridge. The turbulence was frightening. He fought against it in the chrome cubicle but he emerged with one hot, wet trouser leg, regardless. Grabbing at coatsleeves and the occasional head of hair for support, he found his way back to his seat and wedged himself between his large fellow travelers. The two men wrinkled their noses and glanced knowingly at one another, and Thomas Awkner was spared no shame.

All across the continent he sweated. It took time for him to realize that it wasn't only flying that had put fear into him: it was his own curiosity that frightened him. Never before had Thomas Awkner, the courier, experienced the slightest interest in the messages, the mysteries, he bore. What was in the envelope? What did it mean? Why fly across Australia to deliver it in a public place? He longed to take it out of his pocket, hold it to a window, sniff it, rattle it, but these things would draw attention. Whose attention? His newfound curiosity brought fresh fears. Could this mission be *dangerous?* He sweated.

All he could do was deliver something and come back as always, as though a rubber cord anchored him firmly to that asbestos house in the coastal suburbs. But suddenly it seemed difficult. His filtering process was breaking down. When he went back would he still be able to absent himself from the workings of the family? He had learned that skill early on, from the year Aunt Dilly and Aunt Celia had dossed in his room with him. Their snoring, their belches and mutterings, their stockings hanging like jungle snakes and their stares across the curtain as he dressed—these things he taught himself to ignore, and fairly soon all the machinations of the Awkner family happened on the gray, outer limits of his awareness. He did not question the prolonged absences of his brothers and his Uncle Dubbo. He never wondered about the huge unmarked containers their milk arrived in, or the boxes of unstamped eggs, the sudden appearance of a television set. Conspiratorial laughter broke through the asbestos walls like cricket balls, and all those years Thomas Awkner studied the discipline of inertia: he watched little, listened little, said little, did little. His schooling was not superb. He had no friends. And when, quite suddenly, the Awkners left town for Melbourne, he found himself alone with his mother.

2

The airport terminal was confusing: so many escalators and shops and purposeful people, and it was difficult to make headway, always casting looks over one's shoulder. He walked into the women's toilets, had to pay for a box of doughnuts he knocked to the floor, and was dragged from a Singapore Airlines queue and interrogated by customs officers. All he wanted was a taxi, and when he did find the taxi rank, the city of Melbourne seemed short of taxis.

After a wait in the sun, a cab eased up to the curb beside him. He got in.

Pulling away from the rank, the driver asked him where he wanted to go.

"The gallery," Thomas Awkner said.

"What gallery?"

"The art gallery."

"Which one?" asked the driver, getting a good look at him in the mirror. Thomas Awkner was not a settling sight. His fine blonde hair stood up like wheat to the sun; he had not shaved; the flight had left his clothes rumpled. He stank of urine. "Which art gallery, mate?"

"The proper one." He was confused; he hadn't expected this.

The driver shrugged and took a punt and a left turn. "How long you in town for?"

"Two hours."

The driver settled lower in his seat. After all, what kind of man stays in a town for two hours? Not the kind of man you told knock-knock jokes to. He drove faster. Thomas Awkner skated about on the seat of his pants, smitten by the strangeness of the place. The buildings were half buried in trees, their lines were soft and their textures aged. It reminded him of Fremantle where he was born: houses standing shoulder to shoulder, old men walking in narrow streets. It charmed him. It flooded him with memories of walking to the wharf with his father. They lived in Fremantle to make it more convenient to visit relatives in prison. The air was full of gulls and the stench of sheep ships and harbor scum. Some days, Thomas walked with his father to the wharf where they would meet strange men and his father would whisper with them in the shadows of hawsers and derricks. The shimmer of the water's surface tantalized him. He always wanted to dive in. He begged his father to let him paddle at the little beach behind the mole, but there was never time and his father mentioned sunburn and rips and sharks.

"You'll sink like a stone," his father said. They were the only words he remembered from his father.

The taxi stopped with such suddenness that Thomas cracked his chin on the ashtray of the seat in front. It cleared his head for a moment. He paid and got out into the disarming sunshine. He had an hour and a half left. He was to meet Uncle Dubbo here beside the dormant fountain in fifty minutes. It was hot in the sun. The sight of water running down glass attracted him to the building. He went in.

An atmosphere of sanctity was in the place. Tiny lights from heights. A brooding quiet. He decided to wait in there out of the heat until it was time to deliver. He saw his startled face in glass cabinets full of obscure artifacts; he recognized his hooked nose on a Roman bust and his doe eyes in a Dutch oil painting. He saw pieces of himself everywhere. Normally he could not even bear to see his own reflection in the mirror.

It was thirty minutes before he saw the ceiling and when he did, the oddest sensation touched him. Stained glass—acres of it, it seemed. Fremantle. The old church. He remembered. On the way home from the wharf sometimes, he had followed his father into the old church where the sailors went, and he would be left to stand at the back near the door while his father went down toward the sanctuary to speak to men dressed in gray suits with hats in their hands. Often they would come away with little parcels that his father took out to the incinerator later in the day, but while they were speaking, Thomas was mesmerized by the scenes in stained glass at either side of the church. Every candle seemed to point toward the strange characters and their animals. On the way home, Thomas would dawdle behind his father, heavy with wonder.

In the middle of the gallery, Thomas Awkner took off his coat and lay on the carpet, looking up at the canopy of colors. Time passed beyond him as the panels of colored light transported him back. He had forgotten wonder long ago and had replaced it with a dejected kind of bewilderment with which he armed himself to fight off the world from the slit-trench of his unmade bed. In those days of wonder, he had not been repulsed by his own image, he had not been afraid of his own height.

A man stooped and touched him on the shoulder.

"Uncle Dubbo?" If it is Uncle Dubbo, he thought, taking in the man's neatly pressed trousers and blazer and the well-organized face above them, then the plastic surgeons have done a first-class job.

"Sir, you can't lie here all day. There are vagrancy laws in the state of Victoria."

"Oh."

When he got up he saw that he'd left a wet patch of sweat on the carpet in the shape of a man, and by the time he had reached the door of the men's toilet people were noticing it. In the glittering hall of the toilet, Thomas Awkner splashed his face with water and looked at himself brazenly in the vast mirror. He was tall. His thin blonde hair was matted but not entirely disgraceful. His face was lean and his features thin and (perhaps, he thought, it's the heat) even vaguely elegant. The sight drilled him with that odd sensation again.

He heard a shifting sound in the cubicle behind and was suddenly afraid. He touched the manila envelope inside his shirt. He was a courier. A curious courier. Whatever it was he was carrying, he knew, it was important enough to be wanted by someone else. Perhaps everyone else. Thomas Awkner fled the toilet and walked quickly back to the entrance of the gallery, telling himself with fervor: "I've got a mission."

Out under the blinding sun, gelato vans had parked beneath the roadside trees. People sat around the perimeter of the fountain pool. A hot wind stirred deciduous leaves along the pavements and traffic passed, fuming. No sign of Uncle Dubbo. Twenty minutes left, yet. He wondered what he would say to him. A year had passed since he'd seen his Uncle Dubbo, and yet, in all the years through which his uncle had come and gone, in and out of his life, he had never really looked hard at him. Uncle Dubbo never engaged him in conversation. Maybe he'd put the old man through a few conversational hoops before delivery. How bad did he want this envelope? What would he do to get it? What *was* Uncle Dubbo really like? What did he *do* all these years? What about those gray ghosts, his own brothers? He could barely remember them. Maybe, he thought, a few questions might be the price of delivery, this time. Was it really an aerosol can that blew the old man's head off? What does it all mean? What's my life honestly been about, for God's sake?

Thomas took out his return ticket and turned it over. Stuffing it back in his pocket, he bought an ice cream and sat at the edge of the pool. Two small boys tugged their shirts off and made shallow dives into the water, stirring up a sediment of leaves and potato-chip bags as they skimmed along the bottom and came up gasping beneath the NO WADING sign. People clucked in disapproval. Thomas watched the boys, envious. He had put his jacket on again to cover the bulge of the envelope, and the heat was unpleasant. He watched as the boys duck-dived and came up with coins. A woman next to him, long breasted, long faced, crinkled her shopping bags, and rattled her tongue.

"Decent people throw their money in there. To make wishes."

He looked at her. Reflected light from the water was unkind to her face. He opened his mouth to speak, then closed it again. A moment later he came out with it anyway, grinning like a clergyman.

"Well, so will they when they grow old and stupid."

She cut him with a stare and turned away. With their hands full of coins, the two boys ran across the pavement to the ice-cream vans, footsteps evaporating behind them. When they came back with dripping cones and smeared faces, Thomas Awkner was untying his shoelaces. The woman turned to stare at him. He returned her stare and without taking his eyes from hers slipped sideways into the water. She screamed, brushing drops from her dress, while Thomas Awkner struck out across the mucky pool, ice-cream cone in hand, to the cheers of the boys. Cool water rushed through his clothing and he felt like singing. His head cleared and he remembered his father's words. Resting at the end of the pool, he watched the boys finish their ice creams and churn across to where he floated in the shade of the gallery. Behind them he saw the sports jacket and feather-duster moustache of Uncle Dubbo. Thomas lay on his back. He spouted like a whale. He had not been seen. Uncle Dubbo had black eyes. His fists opened and closed as though he might lash out with them at any moment. Thomas recalled suffocating clouds of cigarette smoke, toneless instructions, a plate thrown.

He patted the soggy lump in his shirt. The boys dived around him and he felt the rumor of a laugh in him. The strange city rang in his ears: sound and sight limitless. Uncle Dubbo paced, fists in his pockets. Thomas Awkner floated.

Diesel Epiphany
Thea Astley

THE RAIL-MOTOR IS CROWDED and in our section there are three other people.

We are grouped in twosomes facing each other. We don't know why we're sitting like this. Someone mustn't have bothered to swing the seat back over. Why should they? Nothing else works. The ashtray lids are gone. The windows drop down on your fingers. The blinds don't go up, or if they do, they remain stuck at jazzy angles. In the tunnels the electric lighting proves shy.

The man next to me is asleep. He's been asleep since Tobaccotown. The rail-motor was just about empty then. It's at Mango it fills up with Murris and kids from the youth hostel and a few locals. The backpackers are German and American. The Germans have massive legs, great cameras, and the biggest backpacks in the world. The Americans have meaningful T-shirts with the longest aphorisms.

The man next to me is still asleep. He's missing the two opposite. There's this beautiful young man, medieval-profiled, pallid to the point of illness, looking just like a priest. He's wearing black trousers and a black sleeveless vest over a white shirt. Collarless. His socks are black and so are his shoes. And on his finely shaped head is a bone-colored panama with a narrow black band. It's the panama that gives that final Scott Fitzgerald touch. What a profile, sick or not!

But the girl with him is no Zelda. There's a touch of the nurse, the prefect, despite the Indian smockery. Her clothing looks—well—*dedicated*. Her cosmetic-free face on which the freckles stand out like a sunny day's punctuation is serious and purposeful. You know she'll be into vegetables trees meditation bananas guitars folk and therapeutic sex. That's why he can't be a priest—at least I hope he isn't. She has thick ankles. I see the ankles when she hitches her smock to dump her dilly bag on the floor.

He has thin ankles. The bony projections behind those black silk socks are lumpy with pathos. His eyes are closed. Is he meditating? Maybe he's praying. Maybe he's trying to remember if he bought a ticket. The conductor can't get one from him. His girlfriend has to get off and buy him one while he simply closes his eyes to the whole business.

The rail-motor is held up for four minutes. Some of the Germans glare.

The girl comes back and hands over the pasteboard to be punched.

"Your friend doesn't talk much," the conductor says. He's a curly boy. He's bored with tourists and hippies. Sometimes he hates them because they're not working and sometimes he envies them.

This morning he hates them.

The train hiccups forward.

Outside the windows the scenery is fantastic.

The girl whispers something into the exquisite ear that has crashed onto her shoulder. The conductor moves away in disgust.

The man next to me is still asleep. I wish he'd wake up. I want him to see them, too. I can't take my eyes off them.

Is he a frocked priest, an unfrocked priest, or a frocked un-frocked priest? Is he a teaching brother? Is he simply into black and white clothing? Maybe someone told him he looked like Hurd Hatfield in a panama. He actually looks, now I see him more closely, like a poolroom player somewhat off target.

The rail-motor buckets down the gorge. The scenery is indescribably beautiful. At tunnel twelve the young man is seized with a terrible coughing fit that is close to dry retching. My God, it *is* dry retching. His girl hunts for tissues. There are none. She leans across and cups her hands reverentially beneath his gushing mouth.

Now the man next to me is awake.

He can't take his eyes off them either.

We both can't take our eyes off them.

The girl avoids our faces. She's desperate to get at her dilly bag. A scarf? Something? The young man subsides. She cleans up his face and heads for the toilet.

By the time she comes back, he's ill again. Again the cupped hands. Is he a junkie? (He's a junkie, the man next to me whispers. It's withdrawal.) Is she a masochist?

The train spews itself through tunnel ten.

Outside the windows, the scenery is soul-stirring in its drama but no one's looking at it. The cameras have stopped clicking. I glance round. The whole carriage is riveted on our section. The Americans across the aisle cannot look away.

God, this train is slow!

"Excuse me," the girl opposite says. She eases her companion up and out into the aisle. He really is superb to look at, like a ballet dancer from *Façade*. Even standing there, swaying with his eyes closed. His panama hasn't shifted an inch. Now and again he raises beautifully sensitive hands to check it.

The girl tries to swing the back of the seat over. It's jammed. The young man stands uselessly. I try. So does the man next to me. And the four Americans from across the aisle. The young man sways, shivering slightly, the quiet storm center of monstrous activity.

There's a dreadful grinding sound as the seat back finally turns. The girl picks up her dilly bag from the floor and steers her companion round so that now they have their backs to all of us.

"Some types, eh?" the farmer says to me.

The two in front of us are speaking softly. Is he awake? Is he talking in his sleep? Are they chanting antivomit mantras? By now the train is rattling between cane fields and the heat is billowing in the windows making all of us ill.

In front of us the young man is sick again. I know by the way she moves. It's her hands that come forward, eager almost, for their humiliation. I don't want to see this again. It's as if both of them are de-humanized.

Or is it over-humanized?

Why doesn't she use his hat?

I close my own eyes. There's a silence right through the carriage as if we are serving at a scarifying Mass. Perhaps we are, for when the train pulls in under the big metal roof of Reeftown Station, the detraining is the most orderly I've ever seen. Backpacks are held courteously aside. After you, people say. No, after you.

I walk uptown benumbed as if the day has split open and

I have been tumbled into another dimension, and when I join the queue in the bank I'm unprepared for the ultimate epiphany.

The bank is cool, spacious, tiled. It is also packed, like the train, with ten o'clock tourists and pensioners. We are all orderly. The forms are neatly stacked, the biros work. The lines of customers are patient, passive. Behind their glass windows and steel grilles, the tellers could almost be at prayer.

Suddenly you are aware of disturbance. It's a riot in the air or the mind or the blood. People are looking up, staring about, smiling, frowning.

A strapping young man, tall, discreetly bearded, with clothes as clean-cut as he, is striding at a snapping pace down one side of the huge room, weaving briskly around the tail end of customer queues, between tables, and up the other side, and he is singing in a splendid manly way in a light baritone. The voice is trained. The production impeccable. He looks at no one, though as he passes some start to giggle and others try to pretend he isn't there. He looks so conservative. The tellers, the floorwalkers, the security men ignore him. They also pretend it isn't happening. Has it happened before? Should there be programs, times? Should the bank issue tickets?

I am so delighted, so excited, I would like my transaction to take forever. The queue shuffles forward. One after one. One after one. The singing persists, rising in superb head notes that curve across the high ceiling. What *bel canto!*

Now the laughter has stopped altogether and people are so disconcerted they all pretend, like the tellers, that it isn't happening. Twenties or fifties? the tellers ask. Twenties, people say. They look down, they look away, they fiddle with purses, bags, wallets. But no one can ignore that voice. Or the singer. Who smiles as he strides, not looking directly at anyone, his smile and eye glancing off at the moment of contact, his voice flooding the whole bank.

He's singing words of his own to Bach's secular cantata number 208, *Schafe können sicher weiden*.

Can they all know that? Some are enraged.

Don't they like Bach?

The elderly woman behind me looks up as he swings by.

"You're mad," she says loudly and viciously. "Do you know you're mad?"

Her words sound obscene. I'm ashamed for her. It's as if all the filth she has ever experienced has gathered in her mouth as she vomits out those words.

For I hear *his* words. I hear them phrased and accented to meet the phrases and accents of the cantata.

"Sheep, you're all sheep," he is singing with the best will in the world. "Following like sheep." There are no other words but these. He repeats them, over and over, following the placid geometry of the music through to its resolution. "Sheep, you're all sheep. Following like sheep. Sheep, you're all sheep. Sheep, you're all sheep."

Does anyone else hear? Is this the reason for the anger, the humiliated smiles, the outrage, the pretense of deafness?

For he's right, of course. I have a new and terrible vision of myself.

I tell you, it's made, not my day, but my week month year, maybe my life.

The Old Track

Katharine Susannah Prichard

WHEEL RUTS overgrown with grass and wildflowers, I found the old track, drowsing in sunshine, the other afternoon. But the prickly acacia was in blossom beside it, full of bees, and fringing its swale with living gold.

"The golden road," I thought, and remembered that this was the old track by which hundreds of prospectors had tramped to the Yilgarn goldfields, and beyond them into the unknown interior as far as the Laverton Ranges, of which fabulous yarns are still heard. Who knows what it is doing there?

It looked the wraith of a road winding away over the hills: almost indecipherable among the trees. Yet this was the track the bullock teams and wagons had made as they broke through the scrub and thick timber on their way inland, during the early days, when new land for settlement was sought beyond the barrier of the Darling Ranges.

The Swan River settlement, established in 1829, brought pioneers and their families to the West. A restless young ensign of the 63rd regiment is credited with having led a party across the ranges to where they found the fertile Avon Valley and rich pastoral country for hundreds of miles further on. There, now, the prosperous townships of Northam,

Beverly, and York lie among cleared hillsides with farms, orchards, surrounding them in every direction.

In the old days, the track went on beyond them as far as the Yilgarn Hills, and paused there, daunted by the formidable waterless country that stretched under gray scrub into infinity, it seemed. Six hundred miles from the coast, it took the teams two months to travel the distance.

Then convicts were sent out to construct a road near the old track. They were guarded by soldiers. The ruins of their huts built of mud bricks remain. An old guard house, used by the soldiers, was destroyed by bush fires only a year or so ago.

On the crest of the range, where it overlooks green flats and silver loops of the Swan River meandering by Perth to the sea, an outcrop of rocks marks the spot where a settler and a boy were attacked by natives as they drove through the bush one morning. The boy was speared: the settler escaped; but soldiers surprised the natives and the track was red with blood that day,

For a few years, the road bore the traffic of settlers and pioneers, wagons loaded with stores, men and beasts making the long journey by easy stages to settlements behind the ranges. If any man dreamed of gold in the vast unexplored territories beyond the horizon, his dreams were dissipated when Mr. E. H. Hargreaves, the famous prospector, brought from New South Wales, reported that West Australia was not a country in which gold might be expected to be found except in small quantities.

In 1846 the explorers E. and R. T. Gregory took the track into the unknown and returned without discovering auriferous country.

Again in 1864, Mr. C. C. Hunt, the surveyor, went out along the old road and penetrated four hundred miles beyond the furthest settlement. He described good pastoral land, in the vicinity of the present goldfields, called it Hampton Plains, and started, the following year, with a couple of natives, convicts, and soldiers to blaze a track there.

Three of the convicts escaped. When they were recaptured gold was found in their pockets. They refused to tell where they had found it unless they were given their freedom. That was not conceded, so their secret died with them. Several years earlier, Austin, the surveyor, setting out from Bucklands Farm at Northam traveled as far as Mount Magnet, and came back with wild stories of gold—what might someday be "the richest goldfield in the world," lying out there in the remote wilderness.

The Kimberley rushes brought hordes of old prospectors from New South Wales and Victoria, and in '88 a settler, named Charles Glass, found gold while he was digging a well on his land at Mowjakine. A prospecting party, subsidized by the Legislative Council, searched the district for eight months and reported no gold between York and the Hampton Plains. But other prospectors were making their way out along the old track. They scattered through the Yilgarn Hills and uncovered gold-bearing reefs.

Some old-timers say that Ted Payne struck the first payable gold at Eenuin: others that Tom Risley located a reef thirty miles from Golden Valley and specked the first slug at Cookerdine, which he called Southern Cross, because the stars of the Cross led him and his mates to water when they had been two days without a drop and were likely to perish of thirst. Hugh Fraser had been prospecting further north, but came in and pegged alongside Risley. He got the reward claim and started the mining industry in the Cross with the Fraser gold mine. In a year or so, Yilgarn was booming, and along the old track, hundreds of prospectors tramped, "swamping" beside the wagons that carried their swags and mining gear to the goldfields.

As expectations about Yilgarn faded, disgruntled miners and prospectors followed the track where Hunt had carried it on, or struck out across country from it. Some of them died of thirst: others came in again cheered by traces in the grim ridges whose rocks they had napped and collied. Experienced men believed that the Yilgarn field was only the outer edge of a rich gold-bearing belt inland.

But it was not until '92 that Arthur Bayley rode into Southern Cross, one Saturday morning, with 544 ounces of gold in his saddlebags, and declared a new field 128 miles to the northeast. Next morning the rush had started, and practically all the able-bodied men in the town were surging out along the track leading from the Cross to Bayley's Reward —Coolgardie.

A year later, the track was wandering further east to Hannan's where now the great dumps of the Golden Mile stand with all their poppet legs, derricks, and mine rigging outlined against the sky: the great cities of Boulder and Kalgoorlie encamped at their feet.

By then the railway was crawling out from the pastoral towns. It reached the Cross soon after the trek to Coolgardie began. The old track was being deserted at this end; but I have followed it out from Kalgoorlie, through those end-

less miles of gray scrub, over the shingly red earth to Black
Arrow, Menzies, Gwalia, Leonora, and Laverton, chasing
the byways that run into Kanowna, Kurnalpi, Kookynie,
and back of Leonora to Wiluna.

How did they do it? How on earth did the first prospectors survive in this sun-blasted waterless country? Oh well,
the old-timers say, we went out after rains and made for any
blue hill standing up on the horizon. And camels were a
godsend. Prospecting beyond Coolgardie couldn't have
been done those times, without the camels—and the blacks
who showed us their soaks and gnamma holes.

Beside the track these days stand the ruins of many once-
flourishing mining townships: a few walls of red earthen
bricks and heaps of broken bottles, a pepper tree or two,
with the dumps of a mine in the background, the heaps of
rubble and clay thrown up from shafts and costeens scattered in every direction.

Yet on almost every deserted field, some old fossicker still
lingers, pottering about the dumps or working on an aban-
doned shaft. Usually these old hard-doers maintain that
they are making tucker; but it is not always the weights that
keep them "lousing for gold," as they say, on the site of an
old rush or township that has spent its hour of gay, freak-
ish life and fallen back into the red earth again.

Some of them have made and lost fortunes and gone off
prospecting again because "the country has got them." They
cannot explain the fascination of the gray plains and stark
ridges, their spacious serenity, the sense of immense secrets
held sphinxishly that holds them to this land whose terrifying beauty is so often sterile and pitiless, but soothes them
like a drug with its beguiling peace. I know three old men,

suspected of being "on a good thing," who declare only enough gold to pay their store accounts and give them a spree now and then, because they don't want to sell their mine and destroy the tranquil lethargy of their days.

But there are old mines that have taken a new lease on life since the price of gold soared and working low-grade ores has become a profitable investment.

At Gwalia, the big mine stands on the edge of a salt lake, flanked by a rough red-brown ridge rising from an ironstone plain. The bluff at one end thrusts a black fang against the pale blue of the sky. White huts of the miners clutter the hillside below it like a mountain village in Sicily: here and there are a green trellis, bougainvillea in bloom, goats wandering. Sunset paints the whole place with a rosy glare, and at night the mine buildings nearly a facade, brilliantly lit over the dark plains.

Further along Leonora has two lines of shops, two or three pubs, a church, school, and merry-go-round in the street. Its mines are almost deserted, exhausted; but the track breaks here, one path swinging away to Wiluna, the other to Morgans, which looks as if it had suffered a bombardment, although the mine and cyanide vats on a ridge above continue to function.

All the country roundabout was drought-stricken, a year ago, even the mulga dying. It swept the sky with brown and yellowing brooms, or stood beside the track, withering under red dust.

"Been here for forty years and never seen the country look like this," an old prospector said. "After rains there's green everywhere under the trees, a carpet of wildflowers. Seen the everlastings lying like snow as far as the eye can see."

Away and away, over that dull gray surge of the mulga, a wedge of hills stands up, cobalt, darkening to indigo. As you approach the red slopes throw off their mist. The great dump of the Lancefield mine dominates the countryside like a pyramid. From Laverton to the mine, the track becomes an imposing road that ascends the plateau and disappears among the rows and rows of stark white dog-boxes that are the miners' huts.

Where does it wander then?

Through the oceans of mulga eastward to Lasseter's Reef? The Aborigines may know something of that. A tribe of them drifts past, a forlorn gypsy crew in the faded and gaudy rags of white folks' clothing, men, women, and children, tragic and somber-eyed, an old one-legged gin on crutches.

Here, at its source, the track sleeps in the sunshine. Forgotten. A swale of destiny. It brought hundreds of millions of pounds' worth of gold to light, built cities, changed the face of the country. Many dead towns, deserted mines, derelict miners lie in its wake. Thousands of the men who tramped along it with high hope in the early days have fallen into dust. The dust is claiming almost every young man in the mines of the Golden Mile who works underground for eight years.

But the old rough pathways of life are dwindling away like this track through the bush. New broad thoroughfares will carry our generations into the future, as the Great Eastern Highway, now, bears traffic from Perth to Sydney, past those almost obliterated wheel ruts in the grass.

Postcards from Surfers

Helen Garner

*One night I dreamed that I did not love, and
that night, released from all bonds, I lay as
though in a kind of soothing death.*

Colette

WE ARE DRIVING NORTH from Coolangatta airport.
Beside the road the ocean heaves and heaves into waves
which do not break. The swells are dotted with boardriders
in black wetsuits, grim as sharks.

"Look at those idiots," says my father.

"They must be freezing," says my mother.

"But what about the principle of the wetsuit?" I say. "Isn't
there a thin layer of water between your skin and the suit,
and your body heat . . ."

"Could be," says my father.

The road takes a sudden swing round a rocky outcrop.
Miles ahead of us, blurred in the milky air, I see a dream
city: its cream, its silver, its turquoise towers thrust in a clus-
ter from a distant spit.

"What—is that Brisbane?" I say.

"No," says my mother. "That's Surfers."

My father's car has a built-in computer. If he exceeds the

speed limit, the dashboard emits a discreet but insistent pinging. Lights flash, and the pressure of his right foot lessens. He controls the windows from a panel between the two front seats. We cruise past a Valiant parked by the high-way with a FOR SALE sign propped in its back window.

"Look at that," says my mother. "A WA number-plate. Probably thrashed it across the Nullarbor and now they reckon they'll flog it."

"Probably stolen," says my father. "See the sticker? ALL YOU VIRGINS, THANKS FOR NOTHING. You can just see what sort of a pin'ead he'd be. Brain the size of a pea."

Close up, many of the turquoise towers are not yet sold. EVERY CONCEIVABLE FEATURE, the signs say. They have names like Capricornia, Biarritz, The Breakers, Acapulco, Rio.

I had a Brazilian friend when I lived in Paris. He showed me a postcard, once, of Rio where he was born and brought up. The card bore an aerial shot of a splendid, curved trop-ical beach, fringed with palms, its sand pure as snow.

"Why don't you live in Brazil," I said, "if it's as beautiful as this?"

"Because," said my friend, "right behind that beach there is a huge military base."

In my turn I showed him a postcard of my country. It was a reproduction of that Streeton painting called *The Land of the Golden Fleece* which in my homesickness I kept stand-ing on the heater in my bedroom. He studied it carefully. At last he turned his currant-colored eyes to me and said,

"Les arbres sont rouges?" Are the trees red?

Several years later, six months ago, I was rummaging through a box of old postcards in a junk shop in Rathdowne Street. Among the photos of damp cottages in Galway, of Raj hotels crumbling in bicycle-thronged Colombo, of glassy Canadian lakes flawed by the wake of a single canoe, I found two cards that I bought for a dollar each. One was a picture of downtown Rio, in black-and-white. The other, crudely tinted, showed Geelong, the town where I was born. The photographer must have stood on the high grassy bank that overlooks the Eastern Beach. He lined up his shot through the never-flowing fountain with its quartet of concrete wading birds (storks? cranes? I never asked my father: they have long orange beaks and each bird holds one leg bent, as if about to take a step); through the fountain and out over the curving wooden promenade, from which we dived all summer, unsupervised, into the flat water; and across the bay to the You Yangs, the double-humped, low, volcanic cones, the only disturbance in the great basalt plains that lie between Geelong and Melbourne. These two cards in the same box! And I find them! Imagine! *"Cher Rubens,"* I wrote. *"Je t'envoie ces deux cartes postales, de nos deux villes notales . . ."*

Auntie Lorna has gone for a walk on the beach. My mother unlocks the door and slides open the flywire screen. She goes out into the bright air to tell her friend of my arrival. The ocean is right in front of the unit, only a hundred and fifty yards away. How can people be so sure of the boundary between land and sea that they have the confidence to build houses on it? The white doorsteps of the ocean travel and travel.

"Twelve o'clock," says my father.

"Getting on for lunchtime," I say.

"Getting toward it. Specially with that nice cold corned

beef sitting there, and fresh brown bread. Think I'll have to try some of that choko relish. Ever eaten a choko?"

"I wouldn't know a choko if I fell over it," I say.

"Nor would I."

He selects a serrated knife from the magnetized holder on the kitchen wall and quickly and skillfully, at the bench, makes himself a thick sandwich. He works with powerful concentration: when the meat flaps off the slice of bread, he rounds it up with a large, dramatic scooping movement and a sympathetic grimace of the lower lip. He picks up the sandwich in two hands, raises it to his mouth, and takes a large bite. While he chews he breathes heavily through his nose.

"Want to make yourself something?" he says with his mouth full.

I stand up. He pushes the loaf of bread toward me with the back of his hand. He puts the other half of his sandwich on a green bread-and-butter plate and carries it to the table. He sits with his elbows on the pine wood, his knees wide apart, his belly relaxing onto his thighs, his high-arched, long-boned feet planted on the tiled floor. He eats, and gazes out to sea. The noise of his eating fills the room.

My mother and Auntie Lorna come up from the beach. I stand inside the wall of glass and watch them stop at the tap to hose the sand off their feet before they cross the grass to the door. They are two old women: they have to keep one hand on the tap in order to balance on the left foot and wash the right. I see that they are two old women, and yet they are neither young nor old. They are my mother and Auntie Lorna, two institutions. They slide back the wire door, smiling.

"Don't tramp sand everywhere," says my father from the table.

They take no notice. Auntie Lorna kisses me, and holds me at arm's length with her head on one side. My mother prepares food and we eat, looking out at the water.

"You've missed the coronary brigade," says my father. "They get out on the beach about nine in the morning. You can pick 'em. They swing their arms up really high when they walk." He laughs, looking down.

"Do you go for a walk every day too?" I ask.

"Six point six kilometers," says my father.

"Got a pedometer, have you?"

"I just nutted it out," says my father. "We walk as far as a big white building, down that way, then we turn around and come back. Six point six altogether, there and back."

"I might come with you."

"You can if you like," he says. He picks up his plate and carries it to the sink. "We go after breakfast. You've missed today's."

He goes to the couch and opens the newspaper on the low coffee table. He reads with his glasses down his nose and his hands loosely linked between his spread knees. The women wash up.

"Is there a shop nearby?" I ask my mother. "I have to get some tampons."

"Caught short, are you?" she says. "I think they sell them at the shopping center, along Sunbrite Avenue there near the bowling club. Want me to come with you?"

"I can find it."

"I never could use those things," says my mother, lowering her voice and glancing across the room at my father.

"Hazel told me about a terrible thing that happened to her. For days she kept noticing this revolting smell that was . . . emanating from her. She washed and washed, and couldn't get rid of it. Finally she was about to go to the doctor, but first she got down and had a look with the mirror. She saw this bit of thread and pulled it. The thing was *green*. She must've forgotten to take it out—it'd been there for days and days and *days*."

We laugh with the tea towels up to our months. My father, on the other side of the room, looks up from the paper with the bent smile of someone not sure what the others are laughing at. I am always surprised when my mother comes out with a word like "emanating." At home I have a book called *An Outline of English Verse* which my mother used in her matriculation year. In the margins of *The Rape of the Lock* she has made notations: "bathos; reminiscent of Virgil; parody of Homer." Her handwriting in these penciled jottings, made forty-five years ago, is exactly as it is today: this makes me suspect, when I am not with her, that she is a closet intellectual.

Once or twice, on my way from the unit to the shopping center, I think to see roses along a fence and run to look, but I find them to be some scentless, fleshy flower. I fall back. Beside a patch of yellow grass, pretty trees in a row are bearing and dropping white blossomlike flowers, but they look wrong to me, I do not recognize them: the blossoms too large, the branches too flat. I am dizzy from the flight. In Melbourne it is still winter, everything is bare.

I buy the tampons and look for the postcards. There they are, displayed in a tall revolving rack. There is a great deal of blue. Closer, I find color photos of white beaches, duneless, palmless, on which half-naked people lie on their backs with their knees raised. The frequency of this posture, at random through the crowd, makes me feel like laughing. Most of the cards have GREETINGS FROM THE GOLD COAST or BROADBEACH or SURFERS PARADISE embossed in gold in one corner: I search for pictures without words. Another card, in several slightly differing versions, shows a graceful, big-breasted young girl lying in a seductive pose against some rocks: she is wearing a bikini and her whole head is covered by one of those latex masks that are sold in trick shops, the ones you pull on as a bandit pulls on a stocking. The mask represents the hideous, raddled, grinning face of an old woman, a witch. I stare at this photo for a long time. Is it simple, or does it hide some more mysterious signs and symbols?

I buy twelve GREETINGS FROM cards with views, some aerial, some from the ground. They cost twenty-five cents each.

"Want the envelopes?" says the girl. She is dressed in a flowered garment which is drawn up between her thighs like a nappy.

"Yes please." The envelopes are so covered with colored maps, logos, and drawings of Australian fauna that there is barely room to write an address, but something about them attracts me. I buy a packet of Licorice Chews and eat them all on the way home: I stuff them in two at a time: my mouth floods with saliva. There are no rubbish bins so I put the papers in my pocket. Now that I have spent money here, now that I have rubbish to dispose of, I am no longer a stranger. In Paris there used to be signs in the streets that said, *"Le commerce, c'est la vie de la ville."* Any traveler knows this to be the truth.

The women are knitting. They murmur and murmur. What they say never requires an answer. My father sharpens a pencil stub with his pocket knife, and folds the paper into a pad one-eighth the size of a broadsheet page.

"Five down, spicy meat jelly. ASPIC. Three across, counterfeit. BOGUS! Howzat."

"You're in good nick," I say. "I would've had to rack my brains for BOGUS. Why don't you do harder ones?"

"Oh, I can't do those other ones, the cryptic."

"You have to know Shakespeare and the Bible off by heart to do those," I say.

"Yairs. Course, if you got hold of the answer and filled it out looking at that, with a lot of practice you could come round to their way of thinking. They used to have good ones in the *Weekly Times*. But I s'pose they had so many complaints from cockies who couldn't do 'em that they had to ease off."

I do not feel comfortable yet about writing the postcards. It would seem graceless. I flip through my mother's pattern book.

"There's some nice ones there," she says. "What about the one with the floppy collar?"

"Want to buy some wool?" says my father. He tosses the finished crossword onto the coffee table and stands up with a vast yawn. "Oh—ee—oh—ooh. Come on, Miss. I'll drive you over to Pacific Fair."

I choose the wool and count out the number of balls specified by the pattern. My father rears back to look at it: this movement struck terror into me when I was a teenager but I now recognize it as long-sightedness.

"Pure wool, is it?" he says. As soon as he touches it he will know. He fingers it, and looks at me.

"No," I say. "Got a bit of synthetic in it. It's what the pattern says to use."

"Why don't you—" He stops. Once he would have tried to prevent me from buying it. His big blunt hands used to fling out the fleeces, still warm, onto the greasy table. His hands looked as if they had no feeling in them but they teased out the wool, judged it, classed it, assigned it a fineness and a destination: Italy, Switzerland, Japan. He came home with thorns embedded deep in the flesh of his palms. He stood patiently while my mother gouged away at them with a needle. He drove away at shearing time in a yellow car with running boards, up to the big sheds in the country; we rode on the running boards as far as the corner of our street, then skipped home. He went to the Melbourne Show for work, not pleasure, and once he brought me home a plastic trumpet. "Fordie," he called me, and took me to the wharves and said, "See that rope? It's not a rope. It's a hawser." "Hawser," I repeated, wanting him to think I was a serious person. We walked along Strachan Avenue, Manifold Heights, hand in hand. "Listen," he said. "Listen to the wind in the wires." I must have been very little then, for the wires were so high I can't remember seeing them.

He turns away from the fluffy pink balls and waits with his hands in his pockets for me to pay.

"What do you do all day, up here?" I say on the way home. "Oh . . . play bowls. Follow the real estate. I ring up the firms that advertise these flash units and I ask 'em questions. I let 'em lower and lower their price. See how low they'll go. How many more discounts they can dream up." He drives like a farmer in a ute, leaning forward with his arms curved round the wheel, always about to squint up through the windscreen at the sky, checking the weather.

"Don't they ask your name?"

"Yep."

"What do you call yourself?"

"Oh, Jackson or anything." He flicks a glance at me. We begin to laugh, looking away from each other.

"It's bloody crook up here," he says. "Jerry-built. Sad. 'Every conceivable luxury'! They can't get rid of it. They're desperate. Come on. We'll go up and you can have a look."

The lift in Biarritz is lined with mushroom-colored carpet. We brace our backs against its wall and it rushes us upward. The salesman in the display unit has a moustache, several gold bracelets, a beige suit, and a clipboard against his chest. He is engaged with an elderly couple and we are able to slip past him into the living room.

"Did you see that peanut?" hisses my father.

"A gilded youth," I say. "'Their eyes are dull, their heads are flat, they have no brains at all.'"

He looks impressed, as if he thinks I have made it up on the spot. *The Man from Ironbark*," I add.

"I only remember *The Geebung Polo Club*," he says. He mimes leaning off a horse and swinging a heavy implement. We snort with laughter. Just inside the living room door stand five Ionic pillars in a half-moon curve. Beyond them, through the glass, are views of a river and some mountains. The river winds in a plain, the mountains are sudden, lumpy and crooked.

"From the other side you can see the sea," says my father.

"Would you live up here?"

"Not on your life. Not with those flaming pillars." From the bedroom window he points out another high-rise building closer to the sea. Its name is Chelsea. It is battleship gray with a red trim. Its windows face away from the ocean.

It is tall and narrow, of mean proportions, almost prison-like. "I wouldn't mind living in that one," he says. I look at it in silence. He has unerringly chosen the ugliest one. It is so ugly that I can find nothing to say.

It is Saturday afternoon. My father is waiting for the Victorian football to start on TV. He rereads the paper.

"Look at this," he says. "Mum, remember that seminar we went to about investment in diamonds?"

"Up here?" I say. "A *seminar*?"

"S'posed to be an investment that would double its value in six days. We went along one afternoon. They were obviously con-men. Ooh, setting up a big con, you could tell. They had sherry and sandwiches."

"That's all we went for, actually," says my mother.

"What sort of people went?" I ask.

"Oh . . . people like ourselves," says my father.

"Do you think anybody bought any?"

"Sure. Some idiots. Anyway, look at this in today's *Age*. THE DIAMOND DREAMTIME. WORLD DIAMOND MARKET PLUMMETS. Haw haw haw."

He turns on the TV in time for the bounce. I cast on stitches as instructed by the pattern and begin to knit. My mother and Auntie Lorna, well advanced in complicated garments for my sister's teenage children, conduct their monologues which cross, coincide, and run parallel. My father mumbles advice to the footballers and emits bursts of contemptuous laughter. "Bloody idiot," he says.

I go to the room I am to share with Auntie Lorna and come back with the packet of postcards. When I get out my pen and the stamps and set myself up at the table my father looks up and shouts to me over the roar of the crowd, "Given up on the knitting?"

"No. just knocking off a few postcards. People expect a postcard when you go to Queensland."

"Have to keep up your correspondence, Father," says my mother.

"I'll knit later," I say.

"How much have you done?" asks my father.

"This much." I separate thumb and forefinger.

"Dear Philip," I write. I make my writing as thin and small as I can: the back of the postcard, not the front, is the art form. "Look where I am. A big red setter wet from the surf shambles up the side way of the unit, looking lost and anxious as setters always do. My parents send it packing with curses in an inarticulate tongue. Go orn, get orf, gorn!"

"Dear Philip. THE IDENTIFICATION OF THE BIRDS AND FISHES. *My father*: 'Look at those albatross. They must have eyes that can see for a hundred miles. As soon as one dives, they come from everywhere. Look at 'em dive! Bang! Down they go.' *Me*: 'What sort of fish would they be diving for?' *My father*: 'Whiting. They only eat whiting.' *Me*: 'They do not!' *My father*: 'How the hell would *I* know what sort of fish they are.'"

"Dear Philip. My father says they are albatross, but my mother (in the bathroom, later) remarks to me that albatross have shorter, more hunched necks."

"Dear Philip. I share a room with Auntie Lorna. She also is writing postcards and has just asked me how to spell TOO. I like her very much and *she likes me*. 'I'll keep the sticky-beaks in the Woomelang post office guessing,' she says. 'I won't put my name on the back of the envelope.'"

"Dear Philip. OUTSIDE THE POST OFFICE. My father, Auntie Lorna, and I wait in the car for my mother to go in and pick up the mail from the locked box. *My father*:

'Gawd, amazing, isn't it, what people do. See that sign there, ENTER, with the arrow pointing upward? What sort of a thing is that? Is it a joke, or just some no-hoper foolin' around? That woman's been in the phone box for half an hour, I bet. How'd you be, outside the public phone waiting for some silly coot to finish yackin' on about everything under the sun, while you had something important to say. That happened to us, once, up at—' My mother opens the door and gets in. 'Three letters,' she says. 'All for me.'"

Sometimes my little story overflows the available space and I have to run over onto a second postcard. This means I must find a smaller, secondary tale, or some disconnected remark, to fill up card number two.

"*Me*: (opening cupboard) 'Hey! Scrabble! We can have a game of Scrabble after tea!' *My father*: (with a scornful laugh) 'I can't wait.'"

"Dear Philip. I know you won't write back. I don't even know whether you are still at this address."

"Dear Philip. One Saturday morning I went to Coles and bought a scarf. It cost four and sixpence and I was happy with my purchase. He whisked it out of my hand and looked at the label. 'Made in China. Is it real silk? Let's test it.' He flicked on his cigarette lighter. We all screamed and my mother said, 'Don't *bite*! He's only teasing you.'"

"Dear Philip. Once, when I was fourteen, I gave cheek to him at the dinner table. He hit me across the head with his open hand. There was silence. My little brother gave a high, hysterical giggle and I laughed too, in shock. He hit me again. After the washing up I was sent for. He was sitting in an armchair, looking down. 'The reason why we don't get on any more,' he said, 'is because we're so much alike.' This idea filled me with such revulsion that I turned my swollen face away. It was swollen from crying, not from the blows, whose force had been more symbolic than physical."

"Dear Philip. Years later he read my mail. He found the contraceptive pills. He drove up to Melbourne and found me and made me come home. He told me I was letting men use my body. He told me I ought to see a psychiatrist. I was in the front seat and my mother was in the back. I thought, 'If I open the door and jump out, I won't have to listen to this anymore.' My mother tried to stick up for me. He shouted at her. 'It's your fault,' he said. 'You were too soft on her.'"

"Dear Philip. I know you've heard all this before. I also know it's no worse than anyone else's story."

"Dear Philip. And again years later he asked me a personal question. He was driving, I was in the suicide seat. 'What went wrong,' he said, 'between you and Philip?' Again I turned my face away. 'I don't want to talk about it,' I said. There was silence. He never asked again. And years after that, in a café in Paris on my way to work, far enough away from him to be able to, I thought of that question and began to cry. Dear Philip. I forgive you for everything."

Late in the afternoon my mother and Auntie Lorna and I walk along the beach to Surfers. The tide is out: our bare feet scarcely mark the firm sand. Their two voices run on, one high, one low. If I speak they pretend to listen, just as I feign attention to their endless, looping discourses: these are our courtesies: this is love. Everything is spoken, nothing is said. On the way back I point out to them the smoky orange clouds that are massing far out to sea, low over the horizon. Obedient, they stop and face the water. We stand in a row, Auntie Lorna in a pretty frock with sandals dangling from her finger, my mother and me with our trousers rolled up. Once I asked my Brazilian friend a stupid question. He was listening to a conversation between me and a Frenchman about our countries' electoral systems. He was not speaking and, thinking to include him, I said, "And how do people vote *chez toi*, Rubens?" He looked at me with a small smile. "We don't have elections," he said. Where's Rio from here? "Look at those clouds!" I say. "You'd think there was another city out there, wouldn't you, burning."

Just at dark the air takes on the color and dampness of the subtropics. I walk out the screen door and stand my gin on a fence post. I lean on the fence and look at the ocean. Soon the moon will thrust itself over the line. If I did a painting of a horizon, I think, I would make it look like a row of rocking, inverted Vs, because that's what I see when I look at it. The flatness of a horizon is intellectual. A cork pops on the first floor balcony behind me. I glance up. In the half dark two men with moustaches are smiling down at me.

"Drinking champagne tonight?" I say.

"Wonderful sound, isn't it," says the one holding the bottle.

I turn back to the moonless horizon. Last year I went camping on the Murray River. I bought the cards at Tocumwal. I had to write fast, for the light was dropping and spooky noises were coming from the trees. "Dear Dad," I wrote. "I am up on the Murray, sitting by the camp fire. It's nearly dark now but earlier it was beautiful, when the sun was going down and the dew was rising." Two weeks later, at home, I received a letter from him written in his hard, rapid, slanting hand, each word ending in a sharp upward flick. The letter itself concerned a small financial matter, and consisted of two sentences on half a sheet of quarto, but on the back of the envelope he had dashed off a personal message: "P.S. Dew does not rise. It *forms*."

The moon does rise, as fat as an orange, out of the sea straight in front of the unit. A child upstairs sees it too and utters long werewolf howls. My mother makes a meal and we eat it. "Going to help Mum with the dishes, are you, Miss?" says my father from his armchair. My shoulders stiffen. I am, I do. I lie on the couch and read an old *Woman's Day*. Princess Caroline of Monaco wears a black dress and a wide white hat. The knitting needles make their mild clicking. Auntie Lorna and my father come from the same town, Hopetoun in the Mallee, and when the news is over they begin again.

"I always remember the cars of people," says my father. "There was an old four-cylinder Dodge, belonging to Whatsisname. It had—"

"Would that have been one of the O'Lachlans?" says Auntie Lorna.

"Jim O'Lachlan. It had a great big exhaust pipe coming out the back. And I remember stuffing a potato up it."

"A *potato*?" I say.

"The bloke was a councilor," says my father. "He came out of the council chambers and got into the Dodge and started her up. He only got fifty yards up the street when BA-BANG! This damn thing shot out the back—I reckon it's still going!" He closes his lips and drops his head back against the couch to hold in his laughter.

I walk past Biarritz, where globes of light float among shrubbery, and the odd balcony on the half-empty tower holds rich people out into the creamy air. A barefoot man steps out of the take-away food shop with a hamburger in his hand. He leans against the wall to unwrap it, and sees me hesitating at the slot of the letterbox, holding up the postcards and reading them over and over in the weak light from the public phone. "Too late to change it now," he calls. I look up. He grins and nods and takes his first bite of the hamburger. Beside the letterbox stands a deep rubbish bin with a swing lid. I punch open the bin and drop the postcards in.

All night I sleep safely in my bed. The waves roar and hiss, and slam like doors. Auntie Lorna snores, but when I tug at the corner of her blanket she sighs and turns over and breathes more quietly. In the morning the rising sun hits the front windows and floods the place with a light so intense that the white curtains can hardly net it. Everything is pink and golden. In the sink a cockroach lurks. I try to swill it down the drain with a cup of water but it resists strongly. The air is bright, is milky with spray. My father is already up: while the kettle boils he stands out on the edge of the grass, the edge of his property, looking at the sea.

Stingray

Robert Drewe

SOMETHING MIRACULOUS happens, thinks David, when you dive into the surf at Bondi after a bad summer's day. Today had been humid and grim, full of sticky tension since this morning when he'd spilled black coffee down the crotch of his new Italian cotton suit. He'd had professional and private troubles, general malaise and misery pounding behind his eyes, as he drove home to his flat. He was still bruised from his marriage dissolution, abraded from the ending of a love affair, and all the way up William Street the car radio news had elaborated, on a pop star's heroin and tequila overdose. Then in New South Head Road it warned that child prostitution was rife and economic depression imminent. Markets tumbled and kids sold themselves. Only the coffee stain on his trousers and his awareness of his own body smell prevented him from stopping at the Lord Dudley and sinking many drinks. Instead, a mild brainwave struck him—he'd have a swim.

The electric cleansing of the surf is astonishing, the cold effervescing over the head and trunk and limbs. And the internal results are a greater wonder. At once the spirits lift. There is a grateful pleasure in the last hour of softer

December daylight. The brain sharpens. The body is charged with agility and grubby lethargy swept away.

David swims vigorously beyond the breakers until he is the farthest swimmer out. He feels he could swim forever. He swims onto a big wave, surfs it to the beach. In the crystal evening ocean he even gambols. He is anticipating another arched wave, striking out before it through a small patch of floating weed, when there is an explosion of pain in his right hand.

David stands in chest-deep water shaking his hand in surprise. He's half-aware of a creature camouflaged in the weed scraps and wavelets, on the defensive and aimed at his chest. As he flails away from it into clear water it vanishes. Immediately it seems as if it had never existed and that his demonstration of stunned agony is an affectation, like the exaggerated protestations of a child. But the hand he holds out of the sea is bleeding freely from the little finger and swelling even as he stumbles ashore.

Pain speeds quickly to deeper levels, and then expands. Bleeding from a small jagged hole between the joints, the finger balloons to the size of a thumb, then to a taut, blotchy sausage. Even so, the pain is out of proportion to the minor nature of the wound. This sensation belongs to a bloody, heaving stump. Dripping water and blood, David trudges up the beach, up the steps of the bathing pavilion, to the first-aid room, where the beach inspector washes and nonchalantly probes the wound with a lancet. "Lots of stingrays out there at the moment," he volunteers.

The point of the knife seems to touch a nerve. It's all he can do not to cry out. "Is that what it was?" he asks. His voice sounds like someone speaking on the telephone, mechanical and breathless. The beach inspector shrugs. "I can't find any spine in it." He gives a final jab of the lancet to make sure.

"Shouldn't you warn the swimmers?" David suggests, making a conscious effort to sound normal. He wants to see signs erected, warning whistles blown. He's beginning to shiver and notices that he has covered the floor of the beach inspector's room with sand and water, and a dozen or so drops of blood. He feels ruffled and awry; glancing down he sees one of his balls has come out of his bathers in the panic; he adjusts himself with his good hand.

The beach inspector is dabbing mercurochrome on his wounded finger. On *his* hand a blue tattooed shark swims sinuously among the wrist hairs and veins. He shrugs again. "Stingrays're pretty shy unless you tread on them."

"Not so shy!"

The beach inspector screws the top back on his mercurochrome bottle. "I'd get up to the hospital if I were you," he suggests laconically. "You never know."

By instinct David drives home, left-handed, his pulsating right hand hooked over the wheel. Impossibly, the pain worsens. In Bondi Road he is struck by the word POISON. He is poisoned. This country is world champion in the venomous creatures department. The box jellyfish. Funnel-web spiders. Stonefish. The tiny blue-ringed octopus, carrying enough venom to paralyze ten grown men. The land and sea abound with evil stingers. It suddenly occurs to him he might be about to die. The randomness and lack of moment are right. Venom is coursing through his body. Stopped at the Bondi Road and Oxford Street lights, he waits in the car for progressive paralysis. Is it the breathing or the heart that stops? In the evening traffic he is scared but oddly calm, to the extent of noting the strong smell of frangipani in Edgecliff Road. He knows that trivia fills the mind at the end: his mother's last words to him were "Your baked beans are on the stove." Baked beans and frangipani scent, not exactly grave and pivotal last thoughts.

It would be ironic for such a beach lover to die from the sea. David has known people killed by the sea, three or four, drowned mostly in yachting accidents over the years. He certainly has a respectful attitude toward the sea—as a young lifesaver he even saved a handful of drowning swimmers himself. Thinking back, he has never heard of anyone dying from a stingray sting, unless the shock touched off a cardiac arrest. This knowledge gives small comfort as a new spasm of pain shoots up his arm.

He gets the car home, parks loosely against the curb, and carries his hand inside. He circles the small living room holding his hand. Left-handed, he pours himself a brandy and drinks a mouthful, then, wondering whether it is wise to mix poison and alcohol, pours the brandy down the sink. The hand throbs now with a power all its own and the agitation it causes prevents him even from sitting down. The hand dominates the room; it seems to fill the whole flat. He wishes to relinquish responsibility for it as he has done for much of his past life.

Living alone suddenly acquires a new meaning. Expiring privately on the beige living-room carpet from a stingray sting would be too conducive to mordant dinner-party wit. He considers phoning Angela, his former wife. He imagines himself announcing, "Sorry to bother you. A stingray stung me," and her turning to her new friend Gordon, a hand over the mouthpiece, their gins and tonics arrested, saying, "Now he's been stung by a stingray!" (He never could leave well enough alone.)

She would hurry over, of course. She was cool in a crisis. Gordon would hold the fort. Gordon was adept at holding the fort, perhaps because it wasn't Gordon's fort. This did not stop Gordon from making proprietorial gestures, sitting him down in his old chair and pouring him convivial drinks in his old glasses, when he dropped the children off.

"He's wonderful with the kids," she'd said, driving a barb into David's heart.

He doesn't phone.

He is becoming distracted and decides to telephone Victoria, of whom he is fond. She has mentioned recently at lunch that her present relationship is in its terminal stage and he feels that a stingray mercy dash may not be beyond her.

"Christ Almighty," she says. "Don't move. Sit down or something." In ten minutes she is running up his stairs, panicking at the door with tousled hair and no makeup, and ushering him into her Volkswagen.

The casualty ward at St. Vincent's is crowded with victims of the city summer night. Lacerated drunks rant along the corridors. Young addicts are rushed in, comatose, attached to oxygen. Under questioning, pale concussees try to guess what day it is and count backward from one hundred.

"Please don't wait around for me," David tells Victoria, painfully filling in forms about next of kin. He can barely print. He can't remember his brother Max's address.

"I'll wait," she insists.

As he and his hand are led into the hospital's inner recesses he glances back at Victoria, rumpled and out of kilter, perched on the edge of a waiting-room chair. Their parting seems suddenly quietly dramatic, moving, curiously cinematic. From beneath her ruffled spaniel's hairstyle she smiles anxiously, reflecting this telepathic mood. Rubberized black curtains close behind him.

Among the sea of street and household injuries David's finger is a medical curiosity. A young Malaysian doctor with acned cheeks informs him, "We'll play it by the book." Self-consciously squatting on a narrow bed in an open cubicle, his shoulder blades and buttocks exposed traditionally in a green hospital gown, David is not necessarily relieved.

It was never him in hospitals. It was usually women — having babies, miscarriages, assorted gynecological conditions that owed something to his participation. They always wanted him present. Alone with his unique sting he understands. He lies back holding his own hand.

They inoculate him against tetanus, take his blood pressure, pulse, and temperature readings and a urine sample. They wash and dress the finger and apply a bandage tourniquet to his forearm. "We want to keep an eye on you," says the Malaysian doctor. Around his cubicle the raving of crazed drunks continues. He hears a nurse's voice say, "It's no use, we'll have to put the straps on." A man howls often and mournfully for "Nora." In answer to a nurse's shouted question a concussed woman suggests it is the month of August.

"Close," says the nurse.

"March!" says the woman.

David calls for a nurse and asks whether Victoria is still

in the waiting room. "Please tell her to go home." A moment later she peers through his curtains, enters, sits on the edge of the bed, and holds his good hand.

"You look vulnerable," she tells him, touching his bare back.

"So do you, actually."

"I came out in a hurry."

Amid some commotion four medical staff now wheel an unconscious young woman into the cubicle in front. The staff try to bring her round but the girl, dark-haired and with even, small features, seems to be fighting consciousness. All at once she threshes and moans and tosses her naked body against its restraining straps. "Hilary! Hilary!" the nurses shout. "Come on, Hilary. Be a good girl!"

"What are you still doing here?" David asks Victoria. "It's getting late."

"I want to wait."

"I'm all right. I'm under observation."

"Do shut up."

Hilary is given the stomach pump. The staff attach her to oxygen and various intravenous drips, all the time yelling and laughing in strained camaraderie. Hilary is one of them, their age. Immediately David sees Helena in five, ten years' time, her straight hair, her suddenly longer, womanly limbs, her emotional problems. His pulse beneath the tourniquet throbs almost audibly. "Hilary! Hilary! Do you know where you are!" the nurses sing. His fault.

He and Victoria are silent in sight of this drama. Though the pain doesn't let up he thinks he is getting used to it and feels slightly ridiculous being here.

"Nora, I want Nora," howls the man.

David wants nothing more at this instant than for Hilary to recover.

A violent commotion comes from the girl's cubicle. Suddenly it is jammed with doctors, nurses, and orderlies. The Malaysian doctor is wrestling her, so are two sisters and a nurse. Everyone is loudly swearing and grunting, her bed is shaking, metal clangs and instruments fall to the floor.

"God!" cries David.

They are forcing something down Hilary's throat and mixed up in her gagging and moaning is a cry of outrage and ferocity.

Victoria's hand is squeezing his good one with great pressure. The howling man is muffled by the tumult from the cubicle opposite, now jammed with what seems like the complete hospital staff. Hilary begins to gag again, vomits, and all the staff exclaim and curse angrily. Then they start to laugh. They are all covered in black liquid, the emetic they had forced into her stomach. Hilary has vomited up her pills.

At 2:00 A.M. they release him. Victoria drives him home and keeps him under observation for the rest of the night.

Though the pain lessens next day, six months later the tip of his finger is still numb, the nerve-endings damaged. Victoria, early in their living together, produces one evening a copy of *Venomous Creatures of Australia,* reading which it becomes clear to David that his attacker was most likely a butterfly cod, a small brown fish that looks like a weed.

"They're actually very poisonous," she says generously. "People are thought to have died."

"Let's keep it a stingray," he says.

Ash

Mandy Sayer

WHEN THE AMERICAN sailors surge up the hill from Garden Island to King's Cross in their pressed white suits, they look like one great frothy wave. I sit here at the window when Stub gives me a break and I watch them in their flared pants and spit-shined black shoes, racing each other to the trashy burn of neon along Darlinghurst Road. I watch them tripping over each other and losing their caps and exchanging money. I wonder what exotic place they've sailed from, and how long it's been since they've had a girl.

Not as long as me, I'll bet. I've been waiting all my life.

Sometimes they come up here and pay for it, but not often. They don't have to—whenever there's a ship in, the girls always swarm up here from the suburbs. But the odd times when the sailors do drop by, they're always really well-mannered and I'm polite back to them, just like what Stub told me to be. I do what I'm told. Usually a girl would do my job, but Stub's pretty tight and thinks he can pay a family relation less. Which is true, I guess, since I only get my keep and seventy dollars a week.

Before my mother died, she used to do the work that I do now. No tricks. No, it's all very legit. I sit at the desk and answer the phone. I greet the johns after I've buzzed them through the door. I say to them, So what are you interested in? Like I'm selling shoes or waiting to take their order for dinner, which I guess in a way I am. Sometimes they want a moaner or a punisher, or a girl who'll wrap their bums up in a nappy and talk baby ga-ga, but most of the time they just want big tits or someone who looks pretty in the dark.

I'd like to have someone who looks pretty in the dark, too. Who wouldn't?

My name is Ashley, but everyone calls me Ash. I'm supposed to be in school, reading Slessor and writing essays on Australian poetry. I should be doing my HSC, but Stub reckons it's a load of crap. And after Mum went there didn't seem to be much point.

So I talk on the phone and do a little matchmaking. Early in the morning, after the girls have gone home from their shifts, I go into the rooms and clean them up. I empty the ashtrays and strip the beds. I throw the bottles and cans in the recycling bin. I vacuum. I pick up the used condoms from the floor and throw them away, but I always wear rubber gloves. (A kind of condom for condoms.) And the rooms usually need airing, to get rid of that smell—I don't know what it is. Sex, I suppose. Though Slessor would have called it passion.

I watch them all froth and bubble up the hill in their starched white hats. It's Easter Saturday, and they've all poured out of the *S.S. Independent* for the long weekend. The Americans call it R&R—Rest and Recreation. Though around here we call it Roots and Ruination.

And in comes this guy about my height. There's something about those uniforms that makes those blokes look young and kind of innocent—the square collar and dark blue trim—like little mommies' boys. And I'm thinking maybe he just wants a hand-job or a blow-job, 'cause he's pretty good-looking and could probably walk straight over to The Bourbon across the street and pick up one of those girls from Toongabbie who wear tight Lycra tops and drink Tequila Sunrises and dance dirty down in the basement disco.

But he doesn't. He pulls out this great wad of greenbacks and says he wants a girl for the night.

What do you want? I ask him, like I always do. Meaning, what kind of girl and what turns you on and that.

He says he likes blondes and so I fix him up with Monique (whose real name is Monica—she comes from Parramatta, not Paris). But Monique's shift finishes at twelve, so I make sure he knows little Charlie'll have to fly in and land by midnight. He nods like he doesn't know what I'm talking about, but I reckon he's just bunging it on. I take his three hundred bucks and put it in the drawer. It'll convert to around three hundred and fifty Australian, but I don't tell him that.

During the Second World War, everyone used to complain about the American GIs being overpaid, oversexed, and over here. I guess nothing much has changed.

Once, on a really slow night, I tried to put my arm around Monique's waist—I even offered to pay her, but she just laughed me off and went home.

Not like Charlie and Hook. They're Stub's sons. I don't like calling them my brothers or step-brothers 'cause they're a lot older than me and when one of them takes over my shift they're always late or don't turn up. They never clean up after the girls go home, and always leave a big mess themselves—overflowing ashtrays, empty bottles of Bundy. They've bonked pretty much every girl who's come through here, though Stub'd kill them if he knew. They told me they'd tie me up and cut off my dick if I snitched.

So I send the sailor bloke off to the second bathroom to shower and change into a robe. I knock on Monique's door and tell her he's coming (no pun intended), that he's booked in till the end of her shift. It's only just gone ten-thirty and so I settle down with my Slessor at the desk. After a few minutes I hear the shower stop. He comes out and I thumb him down to the right room.

I try to concentrate on my Slessor, but those guys in their white uniforms keep distracting me. There's a whole group of them out around the fountain. The girls wear loud colors—reds and pinks. They remind me of birds, the kind who grow really bright feathers when mating season comes around. One Yank has this girl in his arms and he's waltzing her across the plaza, spinning her around, and she's throwing back her head and laughing at the sky.

I go back to my book. Monique's already started up. I know her entire repertoire—every sigh and gurgle, every wail. She always starts off real quiet and builds it up, kind of like a musician taking a solo.

Though sometimes I reckon if I hear one more faked orgasm I'm going to start screaming myself.

I read "Cannibal Street," and "Polarities." Then I get up to take a piss. I go into the second bathroom, still steamy from the sailor's shower. After I make my deposit, I wipe the floor down. And as I'm wiping the floor down I see it, the sailor's starched white uniform and cap hanging on the hook behind the door. I finger the crease in the trousers—

so sharp I think I might cut myself. I lift the cap and turn it in my hands. Monique's moaning has just risen an octave, and he's in there, grunting away. I can't resist tucking my hair back behind my ears and putting on the cap. I glance into the mirror. It fits me perfectly, and looks kind of jaunty when I tilt it to the right.

I unbutton my jeans and slip them off. I pull on the flared white trousers with the smart crease, and when I button them up they hug my hips, like they were made for me. It's weird, but it's like when I'm eating a Cherry Ripe and can't stop. I want another because the first one was so good, and so I peel off my T-shirt next and slip into the sailor's shirt. It feels stiff against my skin, like cardboard, but it fits me well, and when I stare into the mirror I raise my hand and give myself a little salute.

The black shiny shoes are a little bit tight, but I can walk in them OK, and the uniform wouldn't look the same without them. It makes me look older, and maybe even better-looking. I turn around and stare at my reflection. I look taller, too. The phone's not ringing and I wonder what it would feel like just to go downstairs for a minute and stand on the street. Just to stand there, wearing all this gear.

Monique's moaning hits third gear. At this rate, he'll get two or three rides by midnight. The shoes squeak as I walk down the hall and let myself out. I creep down the flight of stairs and out onto the footpath. I was just going to stand around and watch the way people look at me, but it feels kind of stupid, and I like the sound of the shoes. Jackie Orszaczky's R&B is blaring from The Bourbon and Beefsteak. I walk past the fish and chips shop and the Astoria Café. The street is swelling with crowds of people. One guy

I know—a friend of Hook's—he's vomiting outside the Westpac Bank. I hurry along past him so he doesn't recognize me.

Japanese tourists are hovering outside the Pink Panther. I scoot around them, listening to the squeak of my shoes. Outside MacDonald's, a pretty girl with long, straw-colored hair is sitting at one of the tables. She's wearing a beautiful long pink dress. I don't know what the material is. Velvet, maybe. She looks up and smiles at me as I pass, and it makes me feel important. I mean, girls never smiled at me before.

I walk down the dirty half-mile, through the blinking neon lights. All I can smell is fried onions from the Korean take-aways. I pass that old, plump hooker who looks like a high-school principal with her hair up in that bun and those cat-eye glasses on a chain around her neck. She asks me if I want a girl, and I say, Yeah, and keep going. I cross the road, and head back. All the barkers outside the strip clubs try to coax me inside. They say things like, Hey, Yankee, why don't you sail in here? The street is dotted with white uniforms, and from a distance they look like big, fat snowflakes swirling down the footpath.

I stop into The Bourbon and Beefsteak to get a packet of Longbeach. I don't usually smoke, but I figure it sort of goes with the uniform. And if I stand here by the bar, drawing on a ciggie, I'll look older than seventeen. The place is really packed. Jackie Orszaczky and his band are playing "Make It Funky," and there are all these navy guys on the dance floor, with hopeful girls in their arms, mouthing the words to the song. I wave around a ten dollar bill and order a Bundy and Coke in my bunged-on American accent. All I have to do is think of Sylvester Stallone in *Rocky*. One dancing navy guy is rubbing his crotch into the belly of a girl with an anchor and a heart tattooed on her left bicep.

I reckon if Slessor was alive today, and was still living in the Cross, he'd write about people like this. People with sweat patches under their arms. Women who spray glitter onto their skin, their faces. Men who get pissed and stick straws up their noses and blow bubbles into their beer when it goes flat.

When the barman asks me if I want another, I shrug and say, Is the Pope a Catholic? That's what Hook always says, and it always sounds pretty cool. I light up another smoke. A few girls are eyeing me from the tables, but I'm just standing here, playing the field.

I down my second one fast, 'cause I should be getting back soon. But the music is getting inside me, underneath my skin, and I can't help swaying from side to side as I smoke.

Then I look up and see her standing in the doorway. That girl in the pink velvet dress, with the long wavy hair. The chick who smiled at me outside MacDonald's. I look away and gaze at the ice cubes in my empty glass. Don't want to look too desperate. When I glance up again, she's on the other side of the bar, ordering a drink. She's got a delicate, heart-shaped face with pale skin and tiny freckles across her nose. She looks familiar, but I don't know why. She doesn't look like she belongs up here. I could see her in a castle, maybe. Or riding in a chariot.

I do my Sylvester Stallone and order one last Bundy and Coke. As I pocket my change, I look up and here she is, right beside me. She's fingering the seam of her dress, real nervous-like. Up close, she looks older than me. Twenty, maybe. And then I hear her voice, real soft, almost a whisper. Would you like to dance? she says. And I can't believe it, 'cause no woman's ever asked me to dance in my life. I guess it's the uniform.

I gulp my drink down. It must be Overproof, 'cause I'm suddenly feeling real dizzy. I hold out my hand and she takes it and leads me onto the dance floor. Jackie's bass is booming all around me. We're underneath a mirrored spinning ball. And I take her into my arms and we start swaying to "In the Dark." She smells of jasmine. I breathe her in. Her hands shift against the small of my back and we're just rocking from side to side. A black navy guy is up on stage with the band, playing harmonica. She's so tiny, so slim, I can feel the curve of her ribcage through her dress. My mouth is wet, and I can't stop swallowing. I've never been this close to a girl in my life, except my mum, of course. And that time I tried to put my arm around Monique and she laughed me off.

She rests her cheek against my chest when the band segues into "I Shall Be Released." I'm stroking the velvet curve of her waist and as the room begins to spin I let it all drain away from me: Stub and his dirty fingernails, the overflowing ashtrays, the used condoms like pale slugs under the beds. My mother gray and lifeless in her rosewood casket. The only life I know is this one pressed against me right now, the one that is soft and smells of jasmine. My hand strays upward and she doesn't stop it. I'm thinking I'll write a poem about this one day. My fingers are shy, but I will them on. And as soon as I touch her breast, she tilts her chin up and parts her pink lips and takes me into her mouth. It feels as if my blood is dissolving. She moves her tongue around inside me, like she's starving for something only I can give her. I'm feeling dizzy again and tighten my grip around her waist.

We go on like this for quite a while. We're not the only ones. There's a guy over near the piano pashing off with a woman in a leather dress. The mirrored ball and all my thoughts glitter and spin. I wonder if I should ask her name or if she wants a drink, but I'm scared. My accent might not come out right.

We're slowly rocking from side to side to "I'm in the Mood." Her hand drops down and cups the left cheek of my arse. I drop mine down and do the same, and it feels as if I'm holding a big warm breast. And I'm thinking about my mother and how much she'd like this girl and how happy she'd be for me if she knew. And I'm thinking about Charlie and Hook, who can only score working girls and chicks who drink at the Football Club. And I'm thinking about what it would be like to lift my hand and unzip her dress, to slide the straps off her shoulders, to slip my hand inside her bra, to press my face into the warm valley between her breasts.

And all of a sudden Jackie stops playing, looks at his watch, and yells at the crowd, *Happy Easter, all you heathens!* And it's only now that I realize what bloody time it is. All I can do is lift this girl's chin up and give her a quick kiss before pulling away and dashing across the dance floor. And already it hurts to leave her. I'm running between the groups of boozers, and I can't bear to look back at her standing alone under the spinning ball. All I know is that it's midnight and Monique's getting ready to go home and young

Popeye has probably wandered back into the second bathroom for his post-bonk shower, and when he gets out, he's
going to be standing there in the raw with nothing to put
on but a bloody plastic shower cap.

I'm running down the steps of The Bourbon, across the
road, weaving between lanes of traffic. A car horn blares and
an old VW nearly knocks me down. If Stub finds out what
I've done he'll tie me down and get one of his mates to tattoo a bull's-eye on my chest. He did that to this guy once
for pilfering the till. I race up the stairs two at a time, unlock
the door, and slip in. I'm expecting a whole lot of yelling and
carrying on, but it's quiet inside. I stand in the foyer and
unzip the shirt and peel it off. It smells of my sweat and cigarette smoke, but I fold it up neatly and straighten the collar, just like Mum would've done. Next the pants. I make
sure I fold them with the crease and lay the shirt on top of
them. I slip off the squeaky black shoes and, in my undies
and socks, tiptoe down the hall. I'm terrified I'm going to
run into Stub. Or Hook, maybe, who can't keep a secret.
And I'm thinking about that bull's-eye and how a needle
must feel, digging into your skin for a couple of hours.
There's no sound of Monique, not even a sigh.

I slip into the second bathroom and lock the door. My
jeans and T-shirt are lying on the floor, where I left them.
Suddenly the door knob starts turning and rattling. I sing
out, *Just a minute!* I pull my own clothes on and hang the
suit back on the hook and place the shoes by the door,
where I found them. I flush the toilet, so it sounds like I've
just been taking a piss. Then I undo the lock.

Sailor boy is standing there in his robe, looking all rosy
and flushed, like they always do when they come out.

Monique's already down the hall, dressed in her spandex pants and top. She gives me a salute and disappears out the door.

I nod to the bloke and let him through. I go back and sit at my desk and gaze outside at all the navy guys clustered around the fountain, jostling each other about and chatting up girls. The shower starts running. I pick up my Slessor and start reading "Mermaids" and "Seafight" and I'm thinking everything is OK, everything is fine. And I get to wondering about my princess in the pink velvet dress and how gorgeous she was and how some other bastard in a white suit is dancing with her now.

Suddenly the sailor comes out dressed in his uniform and squeaky shoes. Where's my cap? he asks, like I'm his mother or something.

My heart goes a bit fluttery. I put down my book and shift in my seat. Well, I say. Well, you're looking for your cap, are you?

He glances around the office, goes back to Monique's room, and comes out again, shaking his head.

Did you, did you have it on when you came in? I ask, all innocent-like.

He nods.

Well, I say again. You know, we've had quite a few of you blokes in on this shift. Maybe, maybe one of your sailor mates picked it up by mistake.

I tell him we're closing now and hurry him down the hall. He keeps stopping all the time and looking about until I tell him we're not responsible for any lost property and bundle him out the door. I lock it and go back to my desk. I can't stop my heart from hammering. I open the second drawer and unscrew the top off Hook's Bundy and gulp down a few mouthfuls. My nerves are just starting to steady. I sit back and take a few more sips. In a minute I'll go down and clean up Monique's room, empty the garbage, and vacuum the carpet. I'll change the sheets, air the room.

I take one last sip and put the bottle away. I'm on my way down to Monique's room when I hear the tinny sound of the doorbell. I figure it's the sailor bloke again and nearly don't answer it. But then I realize Stub might've locked his keys in his car again.

I flip back the lock and the door swings open, and there she is, my princess in pink velvet, her face all knotted up, like she's lost her way. She's standing there, gazing into my eyes like she did only a little while ago beneath the mirrored ball. Her small mouth widens into a smile. And in her hands is the white sailor's cap. She lifts it up to me like it's something precious, a trophy, maybe, or a glass ornament.

You dropped this, she says, on your way out. I saw you come into this building. I wasn't sure if I should come in or not.

She's still smiling at me. I take the cap and, even though I'm just standing here in my jeans and T-shirt, I put it on my head and slant it to the right.

Then I slip my arm around her and pull her inside. Her jasmine perfume has worked its way into my head, my brain. Her lips meet mine and I move my tongue into a soft coil around hers and my blood starts dissolving again.

But then I pull back, kind of guilty-like, and I have to tell her. I take the cap off my head and let it drop to the floor.

I lay my hands on her shoulders, trying to find the right words.

And then I hear her voice, almost a whisper. Do you dress up in army uniforms, too?

My face suddenly feels all hot, and I can't look her in the eye. But she just smiles, and lets out a short laugh. She runs her hand along my cheek and around the back of my right ear.

She says, Your hair's too long for the U.S. Navy.

And then her arms circle my waist again and she puts her mouth on mine.

The White House
Michael Wilding

SO THE OCCASION came to its genteel end. Out in the car park. Finito. Such gentility. Sara has done her best, yelling at the publisher's henchman for pestering her, "Keep your greasy eyes off me," she says, "sexist pig," she adds, for the military chic she wears, khaki overalls or Viet Cong black, the knife-in-the-back paratrooper gear, maybe she doesn't want to be photographed, maybe she doesn't mind being photographed but doesn't want to be pestered. She would spray out a haze of pesticide like a cuttlefish if she could. Maybe that hastened the end. Out into the car park.

"I've got some cans in the car," says Sam.

"He's got some cans in the car," jeers Sara, "what else is new?"

Sam has prised open the door and got out a can and his incisors have latched onto and punctured it and he's happy now, hooked into his mother's milk, and access to a box of more of the same, the six-pack security blanket, the two-dozen off-the-pallet carton, 2 doz. x 350 ml. aluminum bullets, instant relief.

"I'll get in and roll a smoke," Graham said.

But the car park was all a bit public, arts bureaucrats coming and going, talking of David Hockney.

They decided to drive down to Centennial Park and have a smoke, but then they decided that might be a bit unwise, anyway it was probably locked, and then they decided, why didn't they go and park outside the bungalow of the great man of letters, the national treasure, that would be safe, if they parked the other side of the road, surely if the cops picked them up there it would be the fates, the sport of the muses, the mythic absurdity was surely their insurance. So they rolled a smoke in the protection of the home of the great panjandrum, Casa Blanca, the White House.

"It's like sanctuary," said Sam.

"'Sbetter," said Graham.

They rolled another one and smoked it too. And one more. Much better.

A figure appeared outside the bungalow. The place seemed to be floodlit. They couldn't remember if it was like that when they pulled up. The figure descended the flights of steps, came up to the front fence, stood there.

"It's the car," said Sam. "It's a hire car and it's freaking them out, it looks like a police car."

"No it doesn't," said Lily, "it looks like a hire car."

"Yes, that's what I mean," said Sam, "like a hire car." It had Queensland plates, the Sunshine State, glowing there like a little UFO exuding brief bursts of vapor beneath the great fig trees. Sam hired it to deliver copies of his poems round the shops, the back is full of boxes of his new book, it is printed on recycled paper made by monks and bound in parchment made from wood-free human flesh, pig skin, pork crackling, and the paper has the creamy texture of pigs' fat liquefied, ice cream, and the four-color cover has been celloglazed to bring out the depth, and each poem too, so to hire a car to distribute this already phenomenally expensive production, if Sam can be believed, which generally is in doubt, is hardly to add too much to the already impossible bill, so any computation that the cost of the car hire far exceeds anything he can hope to gross let alone net on selling books, his book, this book, is supremely irrelevant. "I'll just keep it till they take it back," he says.

"What's happening, what's he doing?"says Sara.

"I don't know," says Sam.

"What are you going to do?"

There is the snap and hiss of a beer can being opened.

"I don't know," he says.

"We can't just sit here," says Sara.

"I don't know," says Graham.

"What if they call the police?" Sara shrieks.

"That's a point," says Sam.

"I thought you said they thought we were the police," says Lily.

"That's another point," he agrees.

"Go and speak to him," says Sara.

"I don't know about that," says Sam.

"Is it him?" she says.

No, it's not him, the face of a thousand photo calls.

"Who is it?"

"Someone else."

"Who?"

"Go and ask him," suggests Sam.

"We can't just sit here," says Sara.

"I know," says Sam, an idea, "I'll give him a book."

"A book," says Sara. "Just what he's been waiting for.

What an original idea. Why don't you give him a whole box of books? We've got enough."

"I wonder should I sign it."

"We'll all sign it," says Sara.

"No, this is serious," says Sam. He sifts through his pockets looking for a pen. He hasn't got one.

"How can I sign it without a pen?" he asks.

"Here, use this hairpin and write it in blood," says Sara. She prods him with the hairpin.

"Sara," says Sam.

Prod, prod.

"His skin's so thick you can't draw blood."

"You've managed," says Sam.

She keeps prodding him till he gets out of the car.

"Take a book," she says.

He opens the door to get the keys from the ignition to open the boot. Sara prods him some more.

"Fuckin' lay off," says Sam.

"'Fuckin' lay off,'" says Sara. "The poet speaks."

He gets a book and turns toward the white paling fence.

"Isn't anyone coming with me?" he asks.

"No."

"Why are you so nervous all of a sudden?" says Sam.

"The anxiety of influence," says Graham.

"Aren't you coming?" says Sam.

"You're on your own, poet," says Sara.

"We might frighten him off if we all go," says Lily.

"Then you'll have to leave your book on the doorstep," says Sara, "and the dogs will piss all over it."

"Like critics," says Graham.

They sat in the car beneath the fig trees and watched Sam bear his gift across the road. The book is handed over. It is looked at, at arm's length. There are nods, bows. Sam ruffles a hand through his hair. He returns. The figure still stands at the white fence, book held in front of him in both hands, like a sporran. Tribute paid.

"Brave boy," says Sara. "One less to sell."

Sam gets back into the car.

Sara prods him.

"Drive," she said.

Return to Hobart Town

K. C. Koch

THE FIRST SIGHT of the island from the plane causes a leap of the heart, like the sudden appearance of a loved face. All returning Tasmanians experience this. Tugging at its moorings under the giant clouds of the Roaring Forties, Tasmania is different: we are no longer in Australia. All colors have the glassy intensity of a cold climate: the greens greener, the dark blue of the numberless hills and mountains appearing almost black, from the air.

Walking through Hobart at noon, I find that Mount Wellington has snow on its peak, in defiance of summer. The lunchtime crowds in the Elizabeth Street Mall have faces rosy with cold; the red brick paving, puddled from recent rain, is Dutch in its cleanliness; a busker sings "Streets of London." A pair of strolling police officers, male and female, in identical rainproof jackets, have the faces of twelve-year-olds: they look quite incapable of arresting anyone.

The mountain is a constant presence here, guarding the southwest wilderness, looming at Hobart's back. At the city's feet, visible from the mall, is one of the world's best deepwater harbors; but the port is dead. The masts and funnels that crowded it in my childhood, filling me with wild dreams of the world, have gone. The apple boats no

longer load for London; the elegant tourists are no longer
delivered from their giant overseas liners to Hadley's P&O
Hotel. The estuary of the Derwent is vacant and bereft,
staring toward Antarctica.

But the town itself is growing. The population has dou-
bled since my youth, and new suburbs are spreading
through once-pastoral valleys. A few of the witless, multi-
story buildings no community can now escape have
deformed the scale of a once perfectly proportioned colonial city; and in the last decade or so, Hobart has ceased to
be provincial.

This happened with the coming of the gambling casino
at Wrest Point, which was followed by an attendant swarm
of restaurants, coffee shops, and bistros. Many of the restaurants have higher standards than their equivalents in Sydney, and you can now eat *boeuf bourguignon* and Tasmanian
crayfish in tastefully restored Georgian houses, in front of
log fires, served by waiters and waitresses who have time to
be friendly. It makes nightlife in Hobart a vast improve-
ment on the 1950s, when our best choice lay between
Anglo-Saxon hotel dining rooms smelling of old gravy and
the cabaret at Wrest Point for the Sandy Bay rich. But moving along Elizabeth Street, I muse inevitably on what's lost.

The second oldest city in Australia was still in many ways
a village thirty years ago, and the town's patterns were inside
us, unnoted yet constant as the movement of the blood.
Certain passersby (never spoken to, their names never
known) were as inescapable as one's family. And I find
myself still watching out for them. Where is the legless
banjo-player in his wheelchair outside the Ship Hotel?

Where are the two identical spinsters in their 1920's cloche hats? And where is Reggie Wrong?

Our prominent senator and barrister Reggie Wright was well known to the Mainland; but only Hobart knew his counterpart, the other Reggie. Like all villages, we had our favorite fool, and Reggie's nickname was bestowed with cruel affection. Once, at this time of day, he would have been hurrying importantly along Elizabeth Street in his football club blazer, felt hat low over his eyes, arms held out from his plump body like the wings of a stumpy fowl, middle-aged face eager as a boy's. He would strut through Woolworth's and crow like a rooster at the girls behind the counters. They smiled on Reggie with queenly calm in their elegant black frocks, knowing as we all did that a small operation had once been performed on him by the authorities, to make him safe with girls. Or at least, we thought we knew this; perhaps it was a legend.

Many of the old shops have gone, which were here since first settlement. I hear them named in my head by my long-dead grandmother and vanished aunts, their slow voices certain of an unchanging world. "I'll just go down to Mather's." "We'll pop along to Beck's." In Beck's wonderful grocery store, with its adult pungencies of cheese and coffee, my mother and my grandmother would join a row of other matrons on spindly chairs at the counter, formal in hats, suits, and gloves, while a whole platoon of brisk, smiling men in white aprons obeyed their every whim—running up tall ladders to high shelves; checking lists.

At home in our suburb of Newtown, my mother was served by an army of such tradesmen, without having to leave her door: the baker with his basket of bread; the milkman with his rattling cans. And in the winter, the strange figure of the Rabbit Man loomed out of the fog on his horse-drawn cart, with skinned little corpses all strung on wires—crying "Rabby-o!" and ringing his brass bell. Stern-faced as a messenger from the underworld, in his big hat, he was more than a Rabbit Man to me.

The green trams are gone too, and I mourn them. Doubledeckers brought us home from the beach, bucking along like horses. In the open top deck, legs tingling with sunburn, faces cooled by the wind, boys flicked wet towels at each other; and once a splendid madman leaped from the top deck onto the roof of a car below—for reasons that were never explained. The clanging of the trams was like the actual vibration of the town's nerves, and their rails had the significance of journey: silver lines to eternity. Out on the edge of the country, the waiting hum of a tram at its terminus was like the stitch and sound of Time. Grass grew around the foot of the timetable notice board, and if you stirred a pebble, the noise was loud.

Here is Franklin Square, the town's nineteenth-century heart, its big old plane trees out in leaf. I look up at Sir John Franklin and inwardly salute him, as I always do. Chart in hand, the doomed explorer stands on his plinth in the middle of the ornamental pool, a seagull perched as usual on his bald head, which wears a snowy cap of seagulls' droppings. Other gulls wheel and cry about him like the souls of his sailors, lost in the ice of the Northwest Passage. We are fond of Franklin, in Tasmania: he was kindly, and one of our good governors; the information has been transmitted down the generations.

When Franklin and Lady Jane made their overland expedition to the wild West Coast, they were brought back to Hobart on the schooner *Eliza*, under the command of my maternal great-great-grandfather, Captain James Hurburgh, who settled in Van Diemen's Land in 1837. The past is like a trunk in the attic here, very close at hand; ancestors are not far away. Above me, in the square, hover the spirits of two sailors: the famous rear admiral who is still hauntingly lost, preserved in the Arctic ice even now; and a humble merchant captain from Greenwich, who elected to stay on the southernmost edge of the world, and so sealed my fate.

One can walk all over Hobart in a few hours: this town of grandfathers. I am moving today through two earlier Hobarts, their ghostly after-images appearing all the time: the Hobart of the 1940s and my childhood, and the Hobart of the 1840s, and Captain Hurburgh: a sailors' town; a convict town. I wander through the well-preserved nineteenth-century suburb of Battery Point, perched on its ridge above the docks. It used to "bad," in my Depression infancy: a district of grim old poverty, its cottages built for dwarfs. Now it's an expensive film set, full of tasteful paint and coach lamps: a real-estate man's dream. Here are the stone steps built especially for that Homeric whaling master, Captain James Kelly, whose trousers, in response to a bet, were proved to hold five bushels of wheat. Kelly's Steps take me down from the ridge on to Salamanca Place as they once took him; and here is Hobart of the 1840s.

The line of starkly simple freestone buildings along this wharf, erected by convicts, remains the finest colonial group in any Australian port. The buildings went through few transformations until recently; but today, colonial chic is in full bloom. Tamed into preciosity, loved to death, they house craft galleries, coffee bars, and nightspots for tourists with names like "Mr. Wooby's"; and on weekends, open-air markets are set up in front of them.

One shouldn't complain, it's all very pleasant; but it's merely theater, set against the backdrop of an extinct port; and these were once the ship's chandlers and brawling, roaring taverns of the whaling era, when Hobart was "the New Bedford of the Southern Seas." Fortunes were made, and a forest of masts rose beyond the quays: American and European whalers crowded to compete with the Tasmanians. It's recorded that on Good Friday in 1847, thirty-seven foreign whalers (many of them Americans) were refitting at Hobart Town. There was a fast link with San Francisco: ships heading for the gold rush revictualed here, and Hobart merchants supplied the American Pacific coast. The great whale-oil barrels were stacked where middle-aged hippies now ply their wares; sailors flush with money, back from the long trips, drank and fought and found their whores on Salamanca Place. Even twenty years ago, these buildings were still pubs, warehouses, sailmakers, and small factories, whose doorways gave out essential odors of rope, bran, beer, and jam.

In the 1950s, my mates and I drank in the last true sailors' pub here: the now-legendary Esplanade, known as the "Blue House," whose proprietor was the even more legendary Elizabeth ("Ma") Dwyer. Its name meant exactly what it said: if you went in, you had to have a blue: a fight. Most of the clientele were merchant seamen; there were also a few petty criminals and shopworn ladies of the town. Ma's was known from Melbourne to London; but today it's just another example of colonial chic, with a twee sign outside the ground-floor bistro saying "Ma's Bar." None of its present clientele would have ventured inside the old pub.

My friends and I survived in there through cunning, rather than bravery. We bought drinks for the toughest-looking seamen in the bar on our first visit, and when a fight was offered to us by someone else, and a terrible fist thrust under our noses, our friend held up a warning hand. "The boys are with me." We had survived—for a time. Behind the bar, Ma Dwyer presided over the majestic din with absolute authority. Built like a small keg, with dyed orange hair and an expressionless white face by Toulouse-Lautrec, she rarely smiled; but when a Port Line boat was in, she would shout the bar, in memory of her late husband.

She tolerated fighting in the bar within limits; but when it threatened the rudimentary fittings (bare floor; wooden benches) she was capable of throwing the largest sailor out onto the esplanade: and he would let himself be thrown. Ma's rule was unquestioned. One night, two seamen were engaged in combat up and down the stairs outside, and Ma strode out and raised her powerful voice in warning. "I don't mind youse fighting—but *stop bleeding on me stairs!*"

It's pleasant having a cappuccino or a wine in one of Hobart's charming new bistros, and I don't miss the milk bars or basic Greek cafes of the past. But I do miss Ma's.

Mother

Judah Waten

WHEN I WAS A SMALL BOY I was often morbidly conscious of Mother's intent, searching eyes fixed on me. She would gaze for minutes on end without speaking one word. I was always disconcerted and would guiltily look down at the ground, anxiously turning over in my mind my day's activities.

But very early I knew her thoughts were far away from my petty doings; she was concerned with them only insofar as they gave her further reason to justify her hostility to the life around us. She was preoccupied with my sister and me; she was forever concerned with our future in this new land in which she would always feel a stranger.

I gave her little comfort, for though we had been in the country for only a short while I had assumed many of the ways of those around me. I had become estranged from her. Or so it seemed to Mother, and it grieved her.

When I first knew her she had no intimate friend, nor do I think she felt the need of one with whom she could discuss her innermost thoughts and hopes. With me, though I knew she loved me very deeply, she was never on such near terms of friendship as sometimes exist between a mother and son. She emanated a kind of certainty in herself, in her view of life, that no opposition or human difficulty could shrivel or destroy. "Be strong before people, only weep before God," she would say and she lived up to that precept even with Father.

In our little community in the city, acquaintances spoke derisively of Mother's refusal to settle down as others had done, of what they called her propensity for highfalutin daydreams and of the severity and unreasonableness of her opinions.

Yet her manner with people was always gentle. She spoke softly, she was measured in gesture, and frequently it seemed she was functioning automatically, her mind far away from her body. There was a grave beauty in her still, sad face, her searching, dark-brown eyes and black hair. She was thin and stooped in carriage as though a weight always lay on her shoulders.

From my earliest memory of Mother it somehow seemed quite natural to think of her as apart and otherworldly and different, not of everyday things as Father was. In those days he was a young-looking man who did not hesitate to make friends with children as soon as they were able to talk to him and laugh at his stories. Mother was older than he was. She must have been a woman of nearly forty, but she seemed even older. She changed little for a long time, showing no traces of growing older at all until, toward the end of her life, she suddenly became an old lady.

I was always curious about Mother's age. She never had birthdays like other people, nor did anyone else in our family. No candles were ever lit or cakes baked or presents given in our house. To my friends in the street who boasted of their birthday parties I self-consciously repeated my

Mother's words, that such celebrations were only a foolish and eccentric form of self-worship.

"Nothing but deception," she would say. "As though life can be chopped into neat twelve-month parcels! It's deeds, not years, that matter."

Although I often repeated her words and even prided myself on not having birthdays, I could not restrain myself from once asking Mother when she was born.

"I was born. I'm alive as you can see, so what more do you want to know?" she replied, so sharply that I never asked her about her age again.

In so many other ways Mother was different. Whereas all the rest of the women I knew in the neighboring houses and in other parts of the city took pride in their housewifely abilities, their odds and ends of new furniture, the neat appearance of their homes, Mother regarded all those things as of little importance. Our house always looked as if we had just moved in or were about to move out. An impermanent and impatient spirit dwelled within our walls; Father called it living on one leg like a bird.

Wherever we lived there were some cases partly un-packed, rolls of linoleum stood in a corner, only some of the windows had curtains. There were never sufficient ward-robes, so that clothes hung on hooks behind doors. And all the time Mother's things accumulated. She never parted with anything, no matter how old it was. A shabby green plush coat bequeathed to her by her own mother hung on a nail in her bedroom. Untidy heaps of tattered books, newspapers, and journals from the old country moldered in corners of the house, while under her bed in tin trunks she kept her dearest possessions. In those trunks there were bundles of old letters, two heavily underlined books on nursing, an old Hebrew Bible, three silver spoons given her by an aunt with whom she had once lived, a diploma on yellow parchment, and her collection of favorite books.

From one or other of her trunks she would frequently pick a book and read to my sister and me. She would read in a wistful voice poems and stories of Jewish liberators from Moses until the present day, of the heroes of the 1905 Revolution, and pieces by Tolstoy and Gorky, and Sholom Aleichem. Never did she stop to inquire whether we understood what she was reading; she said we should understand later if not now.

I liked to hear Mother read, but always she seemed to choose a time for reading that clashed with something or other I was doing in the street or in a nearby paddock. I would be playing with the boys in the street, kicking a football or spinning a top or flying a kite, when Mother would unexpectedly appear and without even casting a glance at my companions she would ask me to come into the house, saying she wanted to read to me and my sister. Sometimes I was overcome with humiliation and I would stand listlessly with burning cheeks until she repeated her words. She never reproached me for my disobedience nor did she ever utter a reproof to the boys who taunted me as, crestfallen, I followed her into the house.

Why Mother was as she was only came to me many years later. Then I was even able to guess when she was born.

She was the last child of a frail and overworked mother and a bleakly pious father who hawked reels of cotton and other odds and ends in the villages surrounding a town in Russia. My grandfather looked with great disapproval on

his offspring, who were all girls, and he was hardly aware of
my mother at all. She was left well alone by her older
sisters, who with feverish impatience were waiting for
their parents to make the required arrangements for their
marriages.

During those early days Mother rarely looked out into
the streets, for since the great pogroms few Jewish children
were ever to be seen abroad. From the iron grille of the
basement she saw the soles of the shoes of the passersby and
not very much more. She had never seen a tree, a flower, or
a bird.

But when Mother was about fifteen her parents died and
she went to live with a widowed aunt and her large family
in a faraway village. Her aunt kept an inn and Mother was
tucked away with her cousins in a remote part of the building, away from the prying eyes of the customers in the tap-
rooms. Every evening her aunt would gaze at her with
startled eyes as if surprised to find her among the family.

"What am I going to do with you?" she would say. "I've
got daughters of my own. If only your dear father of blessed
name had left you just a tiny dowry it would have been such
a help. Ah well! If you have no hand you can't make a fist."

At that time Mother could neither read nor write. And
as she had never had any childhood playmates or friends of
any kind she hardly knew what to talk about with her
cousins. She spent the days cheerlessly pottering about the
kitchen or sitting for hours, her eyes fixed on the dark wall
in front of her.

Some visitor to the house, observing the small, lonely
girl, took pity on her and decided to give her an education.
Mother was given lessons every few days and after a while

she acquired a smattering of Yiddish and Russian, a little arithmetic, and a great fund of Russian and Jewish stories.

New worlds gradually opened before Mother. She was seized with a passion for primers, grammars, arithmetic, and storybooks, and soon the idea entered her head that the way out of her present dreary life lay through these books. There was another world, full of warmth and interesting things, and in it there was surely a place for her. She became obsessed with the thought that it wanted only some decisive step on her part to go beyond her aunt's house into the life she dreamed about.

Somewhere she read of a Jewish hospital that had just opened in a distant city and one winter's night she told her aunt she wanted to go to relatives who lived there. They would help her to find work in the hospital.

"You are mad!" exclaimed her aunt. "Forsake a home for a wild fancy! Who could have put such a notion into your head? Besides, a girl of eighteen can't travel alone at this time of the year." It was from that moment that Mother's age became something to be manipulated as it suited her. She said to her aunt that she was not eighteen, but twenty-two. She was getting up in years and she could not continue to impose on her aunt's kindness.

"How can you be twenty-two?" her aunt replied, greatly puzzled.

A long pause ensued while she tried to reckon up Mother's years. She was born in the month Tammuz according to the Jewish calendar, which corresponded to the old-style Russian calendar month of June, but in what year? She could remember being told of Mother's birth, but nothing outstanding had happened then to enable her to place the year. With all her nieces and nephews, some dead and many alive, scattered all over the vastness of the country, only a genius could keep track of all their birthdays. Perhaps the girl was twenty-two, and if that were so her chance of getting a husband in the village was pretty remote; twenty-two was far too old. The thought entered her head that if she allowed Mother to go to their kinsmen in the city she would be relieved of the responsibility of finding a dowry for her, and so reluctantly she agreed.

But it was not until the spring that she finally consented to let her niece go. As the railway station was several miles from the village, Mother was escorted there on foot by her aunt and cousins. With all her possessions, including photographs of her parents and a tattered Russian primer tied in a great bundle, Mother went forth into the vast world.

In the hospital she didn't find that for which she hungered; it seemed still as far away as in the village. She had dreamed of the new life where all would be noble, where men and women would dedicate their lives to bringing about a richer and happier life, just as she had read.

But she was put to scrubbing floors and washing linen every day from morning till night until she dropped exhausted into her bed in the attic. No one looked at her, no one spoke to her but to give her orders. Her one day off in the month she spent with her relatives, who gave her some cast-off clothes and shoes and provided her with the books on nursing she so urgently needed. She was more than ever convinced that her deliverance would come through these books and she set about swallowing their contents with renewed zest.

As soon as she had passed all the examinations and acquired the treasured diploma she joined a medical mission that was about to proceed without a moment's delay to a distant region where a cholera epidemic raged. And then for several years she remained with the same group, moving from district to district, wherever disease flourished.

Whenever Mother looked back over her life it was those years that shone out. Then she was with people who were filled with an ardor for mankind and it seemed to her they lived happily and freely, giving and taking friendship in an atmosphere pulsating with warmth and hope.

All this had come to an end in 1905 when the medical mission was dissolved and several of Mother's colleagues were killed in the uprising. Then with a heavy heart and little choice she had returned to nursing in the city, but this time in private houses attending on well-to-do ladies.

It was at the home of one of her patients that she met Father. What an odd couple they must have been! She was taciturn, choosing her words carefully, talking mainly of her ideas and little about herself. Father bared his heart with guileless abandon. He rarely had secrets and there was no division in his mind between intimate and general matters. He could talk as freely of his feelings for Mother or of a quarrel with his father as he could of a vaudeville show or the superiority of one game of cards as against another.

Father said of himself he was like an open hand at solo and all men were his brothers. For a story, a joke, or an apt remark he would forsake his father and mother, as the saying goes. Old tales, new ones invented for the occasion, jokes rolled off his tongue in a never-ending procession.

Every trifle, every incident was material for a story and he haunted music halls and circuses, for he liked nothing better than comedians and clowns, actors and buskers.

He brought something bubbly and frivolous into Mother's life and for a while she forgot her stern precepts. In those days Father's clothes were smart and gay; he wore bright straw hats and loud socks and fancy, buttoned-up boots. Although she had always regarded any interest in clothes as foolish and a sign of an empty and frivolous nature, Mother then felt proud of his fashionable appearance. He took her to his favorite resorts, to music halls and to teahouses where he and his cronies idled away hours, boastfully recounting stories of successes in business or merely swapping jokes. They danced nights away, though Mother was almost stupefied by the band and the bright lights and looked with distaste on the extravagant clothes of the dancers who bobbed and cavorted.

All this was in the early days of their marriage. But soon Mother was filled with misgivings. Father's world, the world of commerce and speculation, of the buying and selling of goods neither seen nor touched, was repugnant and frightening to her. It lacked stability, it was devoid of ideals, it was fraught with ruin. Father was a trader in air, as the saying went.

Mother's anxiety grew as she observed more closely his mode of life. He worked in fits and starts. If he made enough in one hour to last him a week or a month, his business was at an end and he went off in search of friends and pleasure. He would return to business only when his money had just about run out. He was concerned only with one day at a time; about tomorrow he would say, clicking his fingers, his blue eyes focused mellowly on space, "We'll see."

But always he had plans for making great fortunes. They never came to anything but frequently they produced unexpected results. It so happened that on a number of occasions someone Father trusted acted on the plans he had talked about so freely before he even had time to leave the teahouse. Then there were fiery scenes with his faithless friends. But Father's rage passed away quickly and he would often laugh and make jokes over the table about it the very same day. He imagined everyone else forgot as quickly as he did and he was always astonished to discover that his words uttered hastily in anger had made him enemies.

"How should I know that people have such long memories for hate? I've only a cat's memory," he would explain innocently.

"If you spit upward, you're bound to get it back in the face," Mother irritably upbraided him.

Gradually Mother reached the conclusion that only migration to another country would bring about any real change in their life, and with all her persistence she began to urge him to take the decisive step. She considered America, France, Palestine, and finally decided on Australia. One reason for the choice was the presence there of distant relatives who would undoubtedly help them to find their feet in that faraway continent. Besides, she was sure that Australia was so different from any other country that Father was bound to acquire a new and more solid way of earning a living there.

For a long time Father paid no heed to her agitation and refused to make any move.

"Why have you picked on Australia and not Tibet, for example?" he asked ironically. "There isn't much difference between the two lands. Both are on the other side of the moon."

The idea of leaving his native land seemed so fantastic to him that he refused to regard it seriously. He answered Mother with jokes and tales of travelers who disappeared in balloons. He had no curiosity to explore distant countries, he hardly ever ventured beyond the three or four familiar streets of his city. And why should his wife be so anxious for him to find a new way of earning a living? Didn't he provide her with food and a roof over her head? He had never given one moment's thought to his mode of life and he could not imagine any reason for doing so. It suited him like his gay straw hats and smart suits.

Yet in the end he did what Mother wanted him to do, though even on the journey he was tortured by doubts and he positively shouted words of indecision. But he was no sooner in Australia than he put away all thoughts of his homeland and he began to regard the new country as his permanent home. It was not so different from what he had known before. Within a few days he had met some fellow merchants and, retiring to a café, they talked about business in the new land. There were fortunes to be made here, Father very quickly concluded. There was, of course, the question of a new language, but that was no great obstacle to business. You could buy and sell—it was a good land, Father said.

It was different with Mother. Before she was one day off the ship she wanted to go back.

The impressions she gained on that first day remained

with her all her life. It seemed to her there was an irritatingly superior air about the people she met, the customs officials, the cab men, the agent of the new house. Their faces expressed something ironical and sympathetic, something friendly and at the same time condescending. She imagined everyone on the wharf, in the street, looked at her in the same way and she never forgave them for treating her as if she were in need of their good-natured tolerance.

Nor was she any better disposed to her relatives and the small delegation of Jews who met her at the ship. They had all been in Australia for many years and they were anxious to impress newcomers with their knowledge of the country and its customs. They spoke in a hectoring manner. This was a free country, they said, it was cultured, one used a knife and fork and not one's hands. Everyone could read and write and no one shouted at you. There were no oppressors here as in the old country.

Mother thought she understood their talk; she was quick and observant where Father was sometimes extremely guileless. While they talked Father listened with a good-natured smile and it is to be supposed he was thinking of a good story he could tell his new acquaintances. But Mother fixed them with a firm, relentless gaze and, suddenly interrupting their injunctions, said in the softest of voices, "If there are no oppressors here, as you say, why do you frisk about like house dogs? Whom do you have to please?"

Mother never lost this hostile and ironical attitude to the new land. She would have nothing of the country; she would not even attempt to learn the language. And she only began to look with a kind of interest at the world round her when my sister and I were old enough to go to school. Then all her old feeling for books and learning was reawakened. She handled our primers and readers as if they were sacred texts.

She set great aims for us. We were to shine in medicine, in literature, in music; our special sphere depended on her fancy at a particular time. In one of these ways we could serve humanity best, and whenever she read to us the stories of Tolstoy and Gorky she would tell us again and again of her days with the medical mission. No matter how much schooling we should get, we needed ideals, and what better ideals were there than those that had guided her in the days of the medical mission? They would save us from the soulless influences of this barren land.

Father wondered why she spent so much time reading and telling us stories of her best years and occasionally he would take my side when I protested against Mother taking us away from our games.

"They're only children," he said. "Have pity on them. If you stuff their little heads, God alone knows how they will finish up." Then, pointing to us, he added, "I'll be satisfied if he is a good carpenter; and if she's a good dressmaker that will do, too."

"At least," Mother replied, "you have the good sense not to suggest they go in for business. Life has taught you something at last."

"Can I help it that I am in business?" he suddenly shouted angrily. "I know it's a pity my father didn't teach me to be a professor."

But he calmed down quickly, unable to stand for long Mother's steady gaze and compressed lips.

It exasperated us that Father should give in so easily so

that we could never rely on him to take our side for long. Although he argued with Mother about us he secretly agreed with her. And outside the house he boasted about her, taking a peculiar pride in her culture and attainments, and repeating her words just as my sister and I did.

Mother was very concerned about how she could give us a musical education. It was out of the question that we both be taught an instrument, since Father's business was at a low ebb and he hardly knew where he would find enough money to pay the rent, so she took us to a friend's house to listen to gramophone records. They were of the old-fashioned, cylindrical kind made by Edison and they sounded far away and thin like the voice of a ventriloquist mimicking far off musical instruments. But my sister and I marveled at them. We should have been willing to sit over the long, narrow horn for days, but Mother decided that it would only do us harm to listen to military marches and the stupid songs of the music hall.

It was then that we began to pay visits to musical emporiums. We went after school and during the holidays in the mornings. There were times when Father waited long for his lunch or evening meal, but he made no protest. He supposed Mother knew what she was doing in those shops and he told his friends of the effort Mother was making to acquaint us with music.

Our first visits to the shops were in the nature of reconnoitering sorties. In each emporium Mother looked the attendants up and down while we thumbed the books on the counters, stared at the enlarged photographs of illustrious composers, and studied the various catalogs of gramophone records. We went from shop to shop until we just about knew all there was to know about the records and sheet music and books in stock.

Then we started all over again from the first shop, and this time we came to hear the records.

I was Mother's interpreter and I would ask one of the salesmen to play us a record she had chosen from one of the catalogues. Then I would ask him to play another. It might have been a piece for violin by Tchaikovsky or Beethoven or an aria sung by Caruso or Chaliapin. This would continue until Mother observed the gentleman in charge of the gramophone losing his patience and we would take our leave.

With each visit Mother became bolder and several times she asked to have whole symphonies and concertos played to us. We sat for nearly an hour cooped up in a tiny room with the salesman restlessly shuffling his feet, yawning and not knowing what to expect next. Mother pretended he hardly existed and, making herself comfortable in the cane chair, with a determined, intent expression she gazed straight ahead at the whirling disc.

We were soon known to everyone at the shops. Eyes lit up as we walked in, Mother looking neither this way nor that with two children walking in file through the passageway toward the record department. I was very conscious of the humorous glances and the discreet sniggers that followed us and I would sometimes catch hold of Mother's hand and plead with her to leave the shop. But she paid no heed and we continued to our destination. The more often we came the more uncomfortably self-conscious I became and I dreaded the laughing faces round me.

Soon we became something more than a joke. The smiles turned to scowls and the shop attendants refused to play us any more records. The first time this happened the salesman mumbled something and left us standing outside the door of the music room.

Mother was not easily thwarted and without a trace of a smile she said we should talk to the manager. I was filled with a sense of shame and humiliation and with downcast eyes I sidled toward the entrance of the shop.

Mother caught up with me and, laying her hand upon my arm, she said, "What are you afraid of? Your mother won't disgrace you, believe me." Looking at me in her searching way she went on, "Think carefully. Who is right—are they or are we? Why shouldn't they play for us? Does it cost them anything? By which other way can we ever hope to hear something good? Just because we are poor must we cease our striving?"

She continued to talk in this way until I went back with her. The three of us walked into the manager's office and I translated Mother's words.

The manager was stern, though I imagine he must have had some difficulty in keeping his serious demeanor.

"But do you ever intend to buy any records?" he said after I had spoken.

"If I were a rich woman would you ask me that question?" Mother replied, and I repeated her words in a halting voice.

"Speak up to him," she nudged me while I could feel my face fill with hot blood.

The manager repeated his first question and Mother, impatient at my hesitant tone, plunged into a long speech on our right to music and culture and in fact the rights of all men, speaking her own tongue as though the manager understood every word. It was in vain; he merely shook his head.

We were barred from shop after shop, and in each case Mother made a stand, arguing at length until the man in charge flatly told us not to come back until we could afford to buy records.

We met with rebuffs in other places as well.

Once as we wandered through the university, my sister and I sauntering behind while Mother opened doors, listening to lectures for brief moments, we unexpectedly found ourselves in a large room where white-coated young men and women sat on high stools in front of arrays of tubes, beakers, and jars.

Mother's eyes lit up brightly and she murmured something about knowledge and science. We stood close to her and gazed around in astonishment; neither her words nor what we saw conveyed anything to us. She wanted to go around the room, but a gentleman wearing a black gown came up and asked us if we were looking for someone. He was a distinguished-looking person with a florid face and a fine gray mane.

Repeating Mother's words I said, "We are not looking for anyone; we are simply admiring this room of knowledge." The gentleman's face wrinkled pleasantly. With a tiny smile playing over his lips he said regretfully that we could not stay, since only students were permitted in the room.

As I interpreted his words Mother's expression changed. Her sallow face was almost red. For ten full seconds she looked the gentleman in the eyes. Then she said rapidly to me, "Ask him why he speaks with such a condescending smile on his face."

I said, "My mother asks why you talk with such a superior smile on your face."

He coughed, shifted his feet restlessly, and his face set severely. Then he glared at his watch and without another word walked away with dignified steps.

When we came out into the street a spring day was in its full beauty. Mother sighed to herself and after a moment's silence said, "That fine professor thinks he is a liberal-minded man, but behind his smile he despises people such as us. You will have to struggle here just as hard as I had to back home. For all the fine talk it is like all other countries. But where are the people with ideals like those back home, who aspire to something better?" She repeated these words frequently, even when I was a boy of thirteen and I knew so much more about the new country that was my home. Then I could argue with her.

I said to her that Benny who lived in our street was always reading books and papers and hurrying to meetings. Benny was not much older than I was and he had many friends whom he met in the park on Sunday. They all belonged to this country and they were interested in all the things Mother talked about.

"Benny is an exception," she said with an impatient shrug of her shoulders, "and his friends are only a tiny handful." Then she added, "And what about you? You and your companions only worship bats and balls as heathens do stone idols. Why, in the old country boys of your age took part in the fight to deliver mankind from oppression! They gave everything, their strength and health, even their lives, for that glorious ideal."

"That's what Benny wants to do," I said, pleased to be able to answer Mother.

"But it's so different here. Even your Benny will be swallowed up in the smug, smooth atmosphere. You wait and see." She spoke obstinately. It seemed impossible to change her. Her vision was too much obscured by passionate dreams of the past for her to see any hope in the present, in the new land.

But as an afterthought she added, "Perhaps it is different for those like you and Benny. But for me I can never find my way into this life here."

She turned away, her narrow back stooped, her gleaming black hair curled into a bun on her short, thin neck, her shoes equally down at heel on each side.

A Medium
David Malouf

WHEN I WAS ELEVEN I took violin lessons once a week from a Miss Katie McIntyre, always so called to distinguish her from Miss Pearl, her sister, who taught piano and accompanied us at exams.

Miss Katie had a big sunny studio in a building in the city, which was occupied below by dentists, paper suppliers, and cheap photographers. It was on the fourth floor, and was approached by an old-fashioned cage lift that swayed precariously as it rose (beyond the smell of chemical fluid and an occasional whiff of gas) to the purer atmosphere Miss Katie shared with the only other occupant of the higher reaches, Miss E. Sampson, Spiritualist.

I knew about Miss Sampson from gossip I had heard among my mother's friends; and sometimes, if I was early, I would find myself riding up with her, the two of us standing firm on our feet while the dark cage wobbled.

The daughter of a well-known doctor, an anesthetist, she had gone to Clayfield College, been clever, popular, a good sport. But then her gift appeared—that is how my mother's friends put it—just declared itself out of the blue, without in any way changing her cleverness or good humor.

She tried at first to deny it: she went to the university and studied Greek. But it had its own end in view and would not be trifled with. It laid its hand on her, made its claim, and set my mother's friends to wondering; not about Emily Sampson, but about themselves. They began to avoid her, and then later, years later, to seek her out.

Her contact, it seemed, was an Indian, whose male voice croaked from the delicate throat about the fichu of coffee-dipped lace. But she sometimes spoke as well with the voices of the dead: little girls who had succumbed to diphtheria or blood poisoning or had been strangled in suburban parks, soldiers killed in one of the wars, drowned sailors, lost sons and brothers, husbands felled beside their dahlias at the bottom of the yard. Hugging my violin case, I pushed hard against the bars to make room for the presences she might have brought in with her.

She was by then a woman of forty-nine or fifty—small, straight, businesslike, in a tailored suit and with her hair cut in a silver helmet. She sucked Bonnington's Irish Moss for her voice (I could smell them) and advertised in the *Courier Mail* under Services, along with Chiropractor and Colonic Irrigation. It was odd to see her name listed so boldly, E. Sampson, Spiritualist, in the foyer beside the lifts, among the dentists and their letters, the registered firms, Pty. Ltd., and my own Miss McIntyre, LTCL, AMEB. Miss Sampson's profession, so nakedly asserted, appeared to speak for itself, with no qualification. She was herself the proof. It was this, I think, that put me in awe of her.

It seemed appropriate, in those days, that music should be separated from the more mundane business that was being carried on below—the whizzing of dentist's drills, the plugging of cavities with amalgam or gold, and the making of passport photos for people going overseas. But I thought of Miss Sampson, for all her sensible shoes, as a kind of quack, and was sorry that Miss Katie and the Arts should be associated with her, and with the troops of subdued, sad-eyed women (they were mostly women) who made the pilgrimage to her room and shared the last stages of the lift with us: women whose husbands might have been bank managers—wearing smart hats and gloves and tilting their chins a little in defiance of their having at last "come to it"; other women in dumpy florals, with freckled arms and too much talc, who worked in hospital kitchens or cleaned offices or took in washing, all decently gloved and hatted now, but looking scared of the company they were in and the heights to which the lift wobbled as they clung to the bars. The various groups hung apart, using their elbows in a ladylike way, but using them, and producing genteel formulas such as "Pardon" or "I'm so sorry" when the crush brought them close. Though touched already by a hush of shared anticipation, they had not yet accepted their commonality. There were distinctions to be observed, even here.

On such occasions the lift, loaded to capacity, made heavy work of it. And it wasn't, I thought, simply the weight of bodies (eight persons only, a notice warned) that made the old mechanism grind in its shaft, but the weight of all that sorrow, all that hopelessness and lost hope, all that dignity in the privacy of grief, and silence broken only by an occasional "Now don't you upset yourself, pet" or a whispered "George would want it, I know he would." We ascended slowly.

I found it preferable on the whole to arrive early and ride up fast, and in silence, with Miss Sampson herself.

Sometimes, in the way of idle curiosity (if such a motive could be ascribed to her) she would let her eyes for a moment rest on *me*, and I wondered hotly what she might be seeing beyond a plump eleven-year-old with scarred knees clutching at Mozart. Like most boys of that age I had much to conceal.

But she appeared to be looking at me, not through me. She smiled, I responded and, clearing my throat to find a voice, would say in a well-brought-up, Little Lord Fauntleroy manner that I hoped might fool her and leave me alone with my secrets, "Good afternoon, Miss Sampson."

Her own voice was as unremarkable as an aunt's: "Good afternoon, dear."

All the more alarming then, as I sat waiting on one of the cane-bottomed chairs in the corridor, while Ben Steinberg, Miss McIntyre's star pupil, played the Max Bruch, to hear the same voice oddly transmuted. Resonating above the slight swishing and breathing of her congregation, all those women in gloves, hats, fur-pieces, packed in among ghostly pampas grass, it had stepped down a tone—no, several—and came from another continent. I felt a shiver go up my spine. It was the Indian, speaking through her out of another existence.

Standing at an angle to the half-open door, I caught only a segment of the scene. In the glow of candlelight off bronze, at three-thirty in the afternoon, when the city outside lay sweltering in the glare of a blue-black thundercloud, a being I could no longer think of as the woman in the lift, with her sensible shoes and her well-cut navy suit, was seated cross-legged among cushions, eyes closed, head rolled back with all the throat exposed as for a knife stroke.

A low humming filled the room. The faint luminescence of the pampas grass was angelic, and I was reminded of something I had seen once from the window of a railway carriage as my train sat steaming on the line: three old men —tramps they might have been—in a luminous huddle behind the glass of a waiting-shed, their gray heads aureoled with fog and the closed space aglow with their breathing like a jar full of fireflies. The vision haunted me. It was entirely real—I mean the tramps were real enough, you might have smelled them if you'd got close—but the way I had seen them changed that reality, made me so impressionably aware that I could recall details I could not possibly have seen at that distance or with the naked eye: the greenish-gray of one old man's hair where it fell in locks over his shoulder, the grime of a hand bringing out all its wrinkles, the ring of dirt round a shirt collar. Looking through into Miss Sampson's room was like that. I saw too much. I felt light-headed and began to sweat.

A flutter of excitement passed over the scene. A new presence had entered the room. It took the form of a child's voice, treble and whining, and one of the women gave a cry that was immediately supported by a buzz of other voices. The treble one, stronger now, cut through them. Miss Sampson was swaying like a flower on its stalk . . .

Minutes later, behind the door of Miss Katie's sunny studio, having shown off my scales, my arpeggios, my three pieces, I stood with my back to the piano (facing the wall behind which so much emotion was contained) while Miss Katie played intervals and I named them, or struck chords and I named those. It wasn't difficult. It was simple mathematics and I had an ear, though the chords might also in other contexts, and in ways that were not explicable, move you to tears.

There is no story, no set of events that leads anywhere or proves anything—no middle, no end. Just a glimpse through a half-open door, voices seen not heard, vibrations sensed through a wall while the trained ear strains, not to hear what is passing in the next room, but to measure the chords—precise, fixed, nameable as diminished fifths or Neapolitan sixths, but also at moments approaching tears —that are being struck out on an iron-framed upright; and the voice that names them your own.

Pension Day

Archie Weller

ALL DAY THE OLD BLACK MAN SITS, away from everyone else. He wears the same old black coat every day. Once
it had silver buttons and a silk collar and was worn in the
best society with speeches, silver, and champagne.

Now it has no buttons and sits upon the hunched back of
the leader of the redback people. The people who hug the
dark corners and scuttle hideously from rusted hiding place
to rusted hiding place. Away from the pale blue eyes that
are like the sun, burning everything away so all is stark and
straight and true, and there are no cool secrets left.

No one wants to know any of the secrets, anyway.

He sits in the park, the old man, like one of the war can-
nons that guard the perimeter and stick their long green
noses out threateningly at the cars that swish by, not even
knowing they are there. Today's children leap and laugh
over silent steel to further demolish yesterday's pride.

There is no room for yesterday's people.

He is a Wongi from out near Laverton, and he can hardly
speak English. When he first came to Perth many years ago,
he huddled in the back of the police Land Rover and
moaned in terror as the ground swept away before him and
trees and rocks and mountains and towns and his whole

universe disappeared in a blur. Had it not been for the handcuffs around his great wrists, he would have leaped out the door and ended it all then.

The white men had torn him away from his red land's breast for a crime he could not understand.

A life for a life. That was how the law had worked since before everything. The law was the law.

Yet the Land Rover lurched out to the camp and the three policemen had sprung upon him, taking him by surprise as he sat, singing softly, by his campfire.

The dogs had barked, the children screamed, his young girl-woman, already full with a child-spirit, cried, and he had fought with all his strength.

The old men had watched with silent, all-knowing eyes as he was overpowered and two policemen held him while the sergeant clipped on the handcuffs triumphantly.

He took one last look at his night-blackened land and the black shut faces in the red firelight. Rubbed red dust over his horny feet before being pushed gently into the hard, hot Land Rover. A tear slid out of his frightened, puzzled eyes before he closed his mind and hunched into himself.

He was only about eighteen then and although he wore a pair of scruffed grubby moleskins (and an army slouch hat he kept for special occasions) he had only seen white men six times in his whole life.

So that was that.

When he came out of jail seven years later, he was still strong and proud. No one had been able to touch him in there. He had worked all day and at night he had willed himself out over the walls back to his country.

Red dust and thin mulga bushes and glittering seas of

broken glass from the miners' camps. Yellow-sided holes many meters deep. Black open mouths gulping in the hot air and holding white-man secrets and dreams.

Just the place to hide a body snapped in two by powerful hands.

He could never go home again. He would have been killed out at the gabbling, dusty camp, if not by the relatives of his victim, certainly by the new husband to whom the elders would long ago have given his woman.

So he had no country. He had no home. He decided to learn more about the white man's ways that had so awed him.

But what could *he* do? A young man with big muscles, a quick temper, not much knowledge of English—and a black skin? After a few fights in a few country towns, he settled down, working for a produce store deep down south and doing some shearing on the side.

He loved that town. His boss was a good man who protected the angry giant from the taunts that sometimes whipped through the air. It was his boss, too, who found him a good half-caste girl from the nearby mission.

They called him "Jackie Snow" and the name stuck: Snowy Jackson, the straight-shouldered, black colossus among his brown, sharper brethren. There was no love lost between the full-blood and the half-castes. They jeered at the way he worked so hard and refused to share his money around. But they were afraid of his physical and spiritual powers. For wasn't he one from the shimmering emptiness of the desert, a man who came with laws and secrets the brown staggering people had lost or only half-remembered?

He did not tell them that he had lost those, too.

At the produce store he was always cheerful and he kept out of trouble. His educated half-caste wife taught him a little more English, but he never learned how to read or write.

They got their citizenship rights and a little house, just off the track to the town's reserve. Every evening, especially in winter, his wife read the Bible and he stared into the searing heart of the fire with thoughtful, quiet eyes and tried to remember before.

But this was his life now.

At shearing time they put him on the yard work. He loved to stride through the greasy, gray sea, shouting in his own language and clapping his huge hands so they sounded like the echoes from the thunder in the sky above. He would fling his head back and flare his nostrils like a wild black horse, and the sheep would pour into the darkened tin woolshed with a furious clickety-clatter on the wooden grating floor. He felt like a king then, a leader of the people.

The other shearers respected Snowy Jackson for his size and strength. Who else could lift a bleating struggling sheep up above his head and still flash the huge white grin he wore (like his slouch hat for special occasions).

But he used to grow angry sometimes, and picking the stupid sheep up by their shaggy necks he would hurl them into the yard, sometimes killing them.

Then they put him on the shearing team alongside all the white men. He was at last one of them, and he took great pride in his new position. After he got over his first hesitation at the whining shears, he became quite skilled at peeling off the curly wool so it lay, wrinkled and ready, around his feet. Each bald, skinny white sheep that he pushed down the chute was a new piece of juicy fruit for him to chew on, until his belly was full of white-man respect.

Every night when he went home, he would try to explain his joyful day to his little wife, just as once, as a successful hunter, he had recounted his stories to his young woman way away up in the red, swirling Dreaming. But he could not tell the half-caste anything and, after a while, he would stop his broken, happy mumbling and stare into his fire. He would smile softly at things that had happened that day, while the stories came out of his eyes and nestled among the coals so he could see them again the next night.

Dreams, dreams.

One year, his young wife died giving birth to her fourth child.

All her relatives came down for the funeral. They sat around talking and remembering, and catching up on the news. Then they all got back in their old cars and trucks and left.

He just has the rain now, turning the sky gray and the world cold. He used to love the rain. He could stand for hours in the soft drizzle and let all the secrets from the heavy black clouds soak into his soul. But he hated the rain that day, for it was there and his little quiet wife was dead.

He just has the rain—and his tears. All his secrets and the love the half-caste girl had taught him, dripping from his puzzled eyes.

When he was alone, he became roaring drunk and smashed up his house that he and the girl had been so proud of, then went and started a brawl among the Nyoongah people.

He might have been getting older, but his huge angry fists put three of the men in hospital. He was put in jail.

The next morning the boss came and got him out. As he walked down the muddy street in the sultry sun, everyone stared at him, shocked or disgusted at the damage he had done. He followed his boss's footsteps like a huge dog.

So he lost even his pride and gave up.

He worked at the store for a few more years. Every time he thought of his woman he went out and got drunk. He lived in a little humpy in the bush, where no one could find him.

The Community Welfare took away his children one day while he was out hunting. All except the baby, whom Mrs. Haynes the boss's wife was looking after.

He never saw his children again.

He did not shear anymore, as he was getting too old. Beer fat lay over him, like bird dung greening a famous statue.

Just as he had been shearing beside the white men and had gained a type of pride, now he could drink beside white men with another sort of pride. They were all brothers now —getting drunk together.

He left to wander.

He has memories of countless tin-and-asbestos towns with cold white people and whining brown people. He has memories of crowded hotels and fights, and falling asleep drunk in the slimy gutter or under a tree. He tried his hand at boxing on a show-ground troupe. But soon he fell down, forever. His body was left to moulder where it lay, while the laughter bored into him like busy constant ants.

Boys drag lazily past, going nowhere. Cigarettes hang from their thin lips, phallus-like, to prove they are men.

The old man would like to beg for a smoke, but the wine he has drunk today thickens his tongue. All that comes out of his mouth is a thin dribble of saliva that hangs off his scraggly gray beard.

Devils dance out of the boys' black eyes. They swagger, shout, and laugh loudly. The words and laughter are caught by the fingers of the Moreton Bay fig trees. Later, they will be dropped to rot away with the stinking, sticky fruit. But the boys don't know that.

Two peel away from the sly dark group and squat down beside him.

"G'day, ya silly ole black bastard. Gettin' stuck into th' gabba at this time a day? Hey, ya wanna tell us 'ow ya was the state boxer, ole man?"

"Look at the metho 'e's got 'ere, Jimmy."

"Unna? 'E got no sense."

"Look out, Snowman! Featherfoot comin' your way, ya ole murderer."

"Jesus, don't 'e stink, but?"

They laugh.

He smiles, uncomprehending, and nods his head. He knows they are laughing at him. Once he would have leaped to his feet and pulverized the whole group. That was a long time ago, though. He cannot remember.

They steal $20 from him with quick black fingers. They always do, every pension day. Where they had been afraid of his powers before, now they laugh and steal from him. He has no people to look after him. Only himself.

He sits under the tree, surrounded by empty wine bottles. He staggers over to the tap and bumps into two young girls, who shriek and squeal with mirth at him.

"The Snowman's drunk!" they shriek.

Once, they would have had to respect and admire him as he told them about the ways and laws of their tribe.

Once.

Now they have no tribe, and he has no ways.

He half-fills a bottle with water and pours the last of his methylated spirits into it. He sits and drinks, lonely.

He watches as the groups gather in circles. People wander from one group to another or stagger across to the hotel, waiting on the corner. The tribe goes walkabout. They stumble over to the brick toilets, as lonely as he is. They clutch onto the tight circles and pass the drink and words around.

Drink gets hot, words get hot in the cold wind.

The boys strip off their shirts and fight out their quarrels, while the women join them or egg them on.

The people play jackpot or two-up or poker. Some grow rich, some grow poor; almost everyone grows drunk.

Everyone goes home, to wherever home is.

He stays.

The sky gets darker and more oppressive. Then it rains.

First there are the whipcracks rattling across the sky, rolling and growling like puppies playing in the fleeciness of the clouds. The lightning leaps and bounces like children; here, there, and gone. The rain starts off fat and slow but becomes faster and leaner.

He just sits there, finishing off his metho and wishing he

had a smoke. He suddenly vomits up all his pension-day money. All over his coat and face and trousers.

Time to sleep.

The old Aboriginal lies underneath his tree that cannot help him, for it, too, is old and sparse of gentle green leaf. The tree and the man get wet; neither cares, though.

So cold. The rain runs in streaks down his face and body. It washes the vomit off him, with soft hands. The pattering of the rain is interrupted only occasionally by short harsh coughs.

In the early hours of the morning, the cruising police van that, like the gardener, is searching for a few weeds to pull up by the roots and throw in the bin, finds him.

His rain has taken him away from his useless, used-up life. Perhaps back to the Dreamtime he understood.

No one knew the old Wongi was dead until the next pension day.

Life of the Party

Murray Bail

PLEASE PICTURE a pink gum-tree in the corner of a back-yard. This is a suburban gum sprouting more green in the lower regions than usual, and a tree house hammered into the first fork. A stunted tree, but a noteworthy one in our suburb. I live with my wife Joy and two boys Geoffrey and Mark in a suburb of white fences, lawns, and tennis courts. It has its disadvantages. On Sundays drivers persist in cruising past, to peer and comment as we tend our gardens. I wonder what their houses are like. Where do they live? Why do they drive around to see the work done by other citizens? Let me say I am concerned and curious about these things.

Last Sunday was a day of warm temperatures; pure pleasure, really. Tennis sounds filled my ears, and the whine of weekend lawnmowers. There was smoke from burning autumn leaves. I went down to the back of my yard, waited, looked around, and climbed to the tree house.

I am forty-five years of age, in reasonable shape all round. On Sundays I wear brown shorts. Still, it was a climb that was tricky in spots, and then as I settled down the house itself wobbled and creaked under my weight. The binoculars I placed on one of Geoffrey's nails; I moved my weight carefully; I surveyed my backyard and the squares of neighboring houses. Half an hour remained before the party began.

On my left was Hedley's, the only flat roof for miles. He was out the front raking leaves. The sight of rubbish smoke billowing from that tin drum of his made me wonder at lack of thought. We had no washing on the line, but was Hedley's act typical of a nonconformist, the owner of a flat-roofed house? It was just a question. It reminded me of his car (a Fiat), his special brand of cigarettes, his hair which was slightly gray, and his wife, Zelda. Everything she did seemed to begin with Z. An odd game, but true. It was Zelda who owned the street's zaniest laugh, had zealous opinions on the best-sellers, and always said zero instead of the more normal nought or nothing.

In the next house I could see a tennis game. That accounted for the steady plok, plok and random shouts. I trained my glasses on the play without knowing the score. The antics of those people in slow distant motion was quite fantastic. To think that a wire box had been built to dart about in, to chase a small ball in and shout. That was George Watkins. As director of a profitable girdle factory he has an inside story on human fitness. He's also a powerful surfer and when I see him walking he shouts to me, "How you going, Sid?"

The first time I played a game with big Watkins he aced me, and aced me in front of his friends and my wife. Invitations have been received since, but I miss the game to avoid additional embarrassment.

Across the street I could distinguish the drive and the side of Pollard's leafy yard. This is a Cape Cod type of house. As expected Pollard was there, walking up the drive, stopping at plants, hands in trousers, pausing, checking bricks, until he reached the footpath. There, he looked up and down, waiting for mail, visitors, his Prodigal Son, news of some description. He parades the width of his house, a balding figure with a jutting stare like the house.

To my right a widow lives with her daughter. The street was alarmed when Gil died—he seemed to be as healthy as any of us. A short time after, she had a swimming pool dug and tiled and can be heard splashing during days of hot temperature. From my position, as I waited, the waters were calm. Then I thought I saw a man there, lying beneath one of her pool trees, a solid, hairy specimen, on one of those aluminum extension chairs. No? The glasses showed an image of some description. She is wearing slacks, and is blonde and nervous.

Finally, there was the house next door on my right. The binoculars were hardly needed: I was looking down into the weedy garden, and as usual not a soul could be seen. These neighbors are the J. S. Yamas. In three years I suppose I have seen them . . . a dozen times. We have not spoken yet. He has nodded, yes, and smiled, but not spoken. This indifference deeply offends my wife.

"It's wrong the way they don't mix in!"

"Why?"

"Everyone needs neighbors and friends. To talk to."

"Why?"

"You can't live by yourself," she says. "What if something happens?"

That was her frustration as I remember it. Naturally enough, the Yamas' silence made them more and more discussed. The street kept its eyes open. Thinking about it: the

Yamas have a private income; he could be a scholar of some sort; it could be, of course, that one of them is in shocking health, though I doubt it from what I sense of the place. He looks foreign, not Australian, and a fairly decent type.

At that time my yard was silent. Joy was at our beach house with Geoffrey and Mark. I had said to them on Saturday night: "Look, I have to duck up to town tomorrow." Arriving, I arranged the place and made for the tree house. I had raised the venetians and left the screen door open. We have lawn smoothing over most of our yard, and concrete blocks form a path. (I used to say that ours was a two-lawn-mower house—one for the front and one for the back—until people took me seriously.) Halfway between the back door and the tree stands a permanent brick barbecue, tables, and white chairs.

I had invited a dozen or so couples. On the tables I placed plenty of beer, glasses, knives and forks, serviettes, and under Joy's fly-proof net a stack of steaks, sausages, and piles of bread rolls. Tell me a friend of yours who doesn't enjoy a barbecue on Sunday! From Geoffrey's tree house I waited for the guests to arrive. Then a movement occurred on my left. A door slammed, a floral dress fluttered, down my drive came Norm Daniels and his wife. With the binoculars I caught their facial expressions. They began smiling. He adjusted his blue short-sleeved shirt as they neared the front door.

I waited. The Daniels now came around the house, puzzled by the no-answer at the front, seriously looking down the drive; certainly bewildered. Had they arrived on the wrong day? Then, of course, they turned and sighted the barbecue all laid out, and their relief was visible.

Daniels was monk-bald to me as I stared down. He

waited among the tables as his wife called through the back door, "You-who!" She smiled at the fly-screen, then shook her head at the tables and chairs.

"Not there?" Daniels asked.

"They must have gone out for a sec."

He looked at his watch, settled back, and began eating one of my rolls. "Want one?" he asked. She shook her hair. Surrounded by someone else's fresh meat and utensils, she seemed uncomfortable.

Another car pulled up. Daniels went over to the drive. "Down the back!" he called out.

It was Lennie Maunder. About fifty, he was as soft as pork, wore bermuda shorts, and had a bachelor's lopsided walk.

"No one's here," Daniels explained. "They must have gone out for a sec. I'm Norm Daniels. My wife, Joan. Pleased to meet yah. We might as well hang around till they get here."

They sat down and I couldn't catch all their words. It was a distraction trying to listen to them and watch for the next arrival. The word "insurance" floated up to my tree, so I knew Daniels had started on occupations. They were not drinking at this stage, and when Frank and elegant Georgina Lloyd came down they seemed embarrassed, caught as it were, and stood up stiffly, bumping chairs, to smile.

Two more couples arrived, the men with bottles.

"Well," Andy Cheel said, "we might as well have a beer!"

Laughter. The sun was beaming. They began drinking.

The women were seated together, and pecked at the air like birds. I heard Frank Lloyd extroverting into Sampson's ear. Tiny for his name, Sampson was in a bank somewhere, and accordingly gray. Nodding, he said, "This is right. This is right. Yes, this is right."

Lloyd was in advertising and already into his third glass. He blew froth from the top of it. "Ahhh," he said, and half closed his eyes.

The chairs were comfortable, the voices grew louder. Latecomers arrived. Norm Daniels and Lloyd realized they were friends of Ed Canning.

"Come over here, you bastard," they said to him. Lloyd shouted, "Who's the old bag you've got with you?"

"Oh, you!" said Canning's wife. She was quite heavy, but pleased with Lloyd's compliment.

"Have a beer," he said, "Sid's not here yet."

And Bill Smallacombe, who was climbing at Myers, arrived without his wife.

I had a brief mental picture of Joy. In bed one night she sat up and said: "I saw Bill Smallacombe at lunch today with a young girl." She fell back disappointed, full of indignant thoughts; a brown-haired concerned wife is my Joy. As I watched the party I imagined Joy submitting to the sun on the sand, breasts flattened, lying there keeping an eye on young Geoffrey and Mark. She must be satisfied with my career so far and is privately contented when I rush to town on business.

They were all there now, and the drinking had loosened muscles, floated the mouth muscles, wobbling the sincerities. The perils of Sunday afternoon drinking! Ed Canning and Frank Lloyd had taken off their shirts, Lloyd's wife loosened her blouse buttons, familiar back-slapping occurred; laughter, so much laughter. I noticed the bachelor Maunder began stealing beer from someone else's glass. Bill Smallacombe drank heavily and kept going inside to use my lavatory. Clem Emery I could hear repeating the latest stock market prices, and Sampson was complaining that his new concrete path had been ruined overnight by a neighbor's dog.

"What say we get stuck into the grub?" yelled Andy Cheel.

They all crowded forward, chewed on their words, dropping sauce and bones on the lawn, and briefly my name.

"Clear those bottles off the table, Ed, before they fall off," said Canning's wife. She was wearing tight blue slacks.

Carrying four to each hand he lifted the bottles over legs, lawn, to dump them behind the garage. Two were dropped on the last load, and broke with an evil loudness. Someone called out, "He dropped his bundle!" and they laughed and laughed.

Later, Ed's wife said, "You should see their lounge!"

"Those curtains I didn't like," said Georgina Lloyd. "I suppose Joy picked them."

"I've been with her when she's bought stuff that really makes you wonder," said Joan Daniels.

"Where do you think they got to, anyway?" she asked vaguely.

By about half past four the party was noisy. This was emphasized when the Watkins' tennis game suddenly stopped. And from the corner of my eye I caught gray-haired Hedley next door creeping toward our fence. I waited. Hedley squatted down, peered between the planks at the goings-on. He hadn't shaved over the weekend, he twitched his nose, and at one stage scratched between his legs. For a good fifteen minutes Hedley spied before retreating. At his door he said something to his wife, and they went inside. Directly over the road, half-hidden by cars, George Pollard on the footpath faced the direction of our house. The other neighbors were either out or had decided to display no interest at all.

"Only a few bottles left," Cheel announced loudly. "Sid's got Scotch inside, but we'd better not."

"Why not?" asked Lloyd.

There was laughter at that, and I had to smile.

Lloyd touched Canning's wife on her behind. "You old bag," he said. She allowed his arm to go around her neck as he lit a cigarette.

Lloyd later tried a handstand between two chairs, tricky at his middle age, and swung off balance, knocking chairs and breaking glasses. He landed on a pile of chop bones; he lay there sweating, his chest heaving.

"When are you getting your pool?" Georgina asked Clem Emery.

"Say seven weeks. We'll have a bit of a do one night."

"Yes, yes, don't forget us," others shouted.

Then Smallacombe came wandering down to the tree. He stopped right at the foot, kicked a tin, grunted, and loudly urinated. The others glanced vaguely. Sampson turned, but it did seem natural enough, relieving yourself against a gum tree on a Sunday afternoon.

Frank Lloyd, trying to balance a bottle on the hairs of one arm, was pulled away by his wife. "Come on, darl. We must be off." She called to the rest, "We'll be seeing you."

"Gawd, it's twenty past six."

The Daniels moved out with the Lloyds.

"What about this mess?"

"She'll be right."

Smallacombe belched.

"Leave it."

My tree was drafty. They had me bored. I wanted them to go, to leave my place. Why do they linger, sitting about?

Gradually they gathered sunglasses, car keys, their cardigans and handbags, and drifted up the drive in a sad fashion as if they were leaving a beach.

At the gate Ed Canning stopped and shouted, "I've never been so drunk in all my life!" It was a voice of announcement, sincere, and clearly loud enough to reach my tree. My binoculars showed middle-aged, sunglassed Canning rigid with seriousness after his statement. Canning, the manager saving for boat and beach house; his wife had begun yoga classes.

Finally, there was the accelerating procession of shining sedans, saloons, station wagons, stretching past my house. Most of them I noticed had tow bars fitted. Canning, Smallacombe, Cheel, Emery, Sampson, Maunder, etc. One of them sounded his horn three, four times in passing. Was it Smallacombe? He was one of my friends. A stillness occurred, a familiar hour was beginning, lights flickered. And sliding down the tree I had to think about: who would have sounded his horn at me?

American Dreams

Peter Carey

NO ONE CAN, to this day, remember what it was we did to offend him. Dyer the butcher remembers a day when he gave him the wrong meat and another day when he served someone else first by mistake. Often when Dyer gets drunk he recalls this day and curses himself for his foolishness. But no one seriously believes that it was Dyer who offended him.

But one of us did something. We slighted him terribly in some way, this small meek man with the rimless glasses and neat suit who used to smile so nicely at us all. We thought, I suppose, he was a bit of a fool, and sometimes he was so quiet and gray that we ignored him, forgetting he was there at all.

When I was a boy I often stole apples from the trees at his house up in Mason's Lane. He often saw me. No, that's not correct. Let me say I often sensed that he saw me. I sensed him peering out from behind the lace curtains of his house. And I was not the only one. Many of us came to take his apples, alone and in groups, and it is possible that he chose to exact payment for all these apples in his own peculiar way.

Yet I am sure it wasn't the apples.

What has happened is that we all, all eight hundred of us, have come to remember small transgressions against Mr. Gleason who once lived among us.

My father, who has never borne malice against a single living creature, still believes that Gleason meant to do us well, that he loved the town more than any of us. My father says we have treated the town badly in our minds. We have used it, this little valley, as nothing more than a stopping place. Somewhere on the way to somewhere else. Even those of us who have been here many years have never taken the town seriously. Oh yes, the place is pretty. The hills are green and the woods thick. The stream is full of fish. But it is not where we would rather be.

For years we have watched the films at the Roxy and dreamed, if not of America, then at least of our capital city. For our own town, my father says, we have nothing but contempt. We have treated it badly, like a whore. We have cut down the giant shady trees in the main street to make doors for the schoolhouse and seats for the football pavilion. We have left big holes all over the countryside from which we have taken brown coal and given back nothing.

The commercial travelers who buy fish and chips at George the Greek's care for us more than we do, because we all have dreams of the big city, of wealth, of modern houses, of big motorcars: American dreams, my father has called them.

Although my father ran a petrol station he was also an inventor. He sat in his office all day drawing strange pieces of equipment on the back of delivery dockets. Every spare piece of paper in the house was covered with these little drawings and my mother would always be very careful about throwing away any piece of paper no matter how small. She would look on both sides of any piece of paper very carefully and always preserved any that had so much as a pencil mark.

I think it was because of this that my father felt that he understood Gleason. He never said as much, but he inferred that he understood Gleason because he, too, was concerned with similar problems. My father was working on plans for a giant gravel crusher, but occasionally he would become distracted and become interested in something else.

There was, for instance, the time when Dyer the butcher bought a new bicycle with gears, and for a while my father talked of nothing else but the gears. Often I would see him across the road squatting down beside Dyer's bicycle as if he were talking to it.

We all rode bicycles because we didn't have the money for anything better. My father did have an old Chevy truck, but he rarely used it and it occurs to me now that it might have had some mechanical problem that was impossible to solve, or perhaps it was just that he was saving it, not wishing to wear it out all at once. Normally, he went everywhere on his bicycle and, when I was younger, he carried me on the crossbar, both of us dismounting to trudge up the hills that led into and out of the main street. It was a common sight in our town to see people pushing bicycles. They were as much a burden as a means of transport.

Gleason also had his bicycle and every lunchtime he pushed and pedaled it home from the shire offices to his little weatherboard house out at Mason's Lane. It was a three-mile ride and people said that he went home for lunch because he was fussy and wouldn't eat either his wife's sandwiches or the hot meal available at Mrs. Lessing's cafe.

But while Gleason pedaled and pushed his bicycle to and from the shire offices everything in our town proceeded as normal. It was only when he retired that things began to go wrong.

Because it was then that Mr. Gleason started supervising the building of the wall around the two-acre plot up on Bald Hill. He paid too much for this land. He bought it from Johnny Weeks, who now, I am sure, believes the whole episode was his fault, firstly for cheating Gleason, secondly for selling him the land at all. But Gleason hired some Chinese and set to work to build his wall. It was then that we knew that we'd offended him. My father rode all the way out to Bald Hill and tried to talk Mr. Gleason out of his wall. He said there was no need for us to build walls. That no one wished to spy on Mr. Gleason or whatever he wished to do on Bald Hill. He said no one was in the least bit interested in Mr. Gleason. Mr. Gleason, neat in a new sports coat, polished his glasses and smiled vaguely at his feet. Bicycling back, my father thought that he had gone too far. Of course we had an interest in Mr. Gleason. He pedaled back and asked him to attend a dance that was to be held on the next Friday, but Mr. Gleason said he didn't dance.

"Oh well," my father said, "any time, just drop over."

Mr. Gleason went back to supervising his family of Chinese laborers on his wall.

Bald Hill towered high above the town and from my father's small filling station you could sit and watch the wall going up. It was an interesting sight. I watched it for two years, while I waited for customers who rarely came. After school and on Saturdays I had all the time in the world to watch the agonizing progress of Mr. Gleason's wall. It was as painful as a clock. Sometimes I could see the Chinese laborers running at a jog-trot carrying bricks on long wooden planks. The hill was bare, and on this bareness Mr. Gleason was, for some reason, building a wall.

In the beginning people thought it peculiar that someone would build such a big wall on Bald Hill. The only thing to recommend Bald Hill was the view of the town, and Mr. Gleason was building a wall that denied that view. The topsoil was thin and bare clay showed through in places. Nothing would ever grow there. Everyone assumed that Gleason had simply gone mad, and after the initial interest they accepted his madness as they accepted his wall and as they accepted Bald Hill itself.

Occasionally someone would pull in for petrol at my father's filling station and ask about the wall and my father would shrug and I would see, once more, the strangeness of it.

"A house?" the stranger would ask. "Up on that hill?"

"No," my father would say, "chap named Gleason is building a wall."

And the strangers would want to know why, and my father would shrug and look up at Bald Hill once more. "Damned if I know," he'd say.

Gleason still lived in his old house at Mason's Lane. It was a plain weatherboard house with a rose garden at the front, a vegetable garden down the side, and an orchard at the back.

At night we kids would sometimes ride out to Bald Hill

on our bicycles. It was an agonizing, muscle-twitching ride, the worst part of which was a steep, unmade road up which we finally pushed our bikes, our lungs rasping in the night air. When we arrived we found nothing but walls. Once we broke down some of the brickwork and another time we threw stones at the tents where the Chinese laborers slept. Thus we expressed our frustration at this inexplicable thing.

The wall must have been finished on the day before my twelfth birthday. I remember going on a picnic birthday party up to Eleven Mile Creek and we lit a fire and cooked chops at a bend in the river from where it was possible to see the walls on Bald Hill. I remember standing with a hot chop in my hand and someone saying, "Look, they're leaving!"

We stood on the creekbed and watched the Chinese laborers walking their bicycles slowly down the hill. Someone said they were going to build a chimney up at the mine at A.1, and certainly there is a large brick chimney there now, so I suppose they built it.

When the word spread that the walls were finished most of the town went up to look. They walked around the four walls, which were as interesting as any other brick walls. They stood in front of the big wooden gates and tried to peer through, but all they could see was a small blind wall that had obviously been constructed for this special purpose. The walls themselves were ten feet high and topped with broken glass and barbed wire. When it became obvious that we were not going to discover the contents of the enclosure, we all gave up and went home.

Mr. Gleason had long since stopped coming into town. His wife came instead, wheeling a pram down from

Mason's Lane to Main Street and filling it with groceries and meat (they never bought vegetables, they grew their own) and wheeling it back to Mason's Lane. Sometimes you would see her standing with the pram halfway up the Gell Street hill. Just standing there, catching her breath. No one asked her about the wall. They knew she wasn't responsible for the wall and they felt sorry for her, having to bear the burden of the pram and her husband's madness. Even when she began to visit Dixon's hardware and buy plaster of paris and tins of paint and waterproofing compound, no one asked her what these things were for. She had a way of averting her eyes that indicated her terror of questions. Old Dixon carried the plaster of paris and the tins of paint out to her pram for her and watched her push them away. "Poor woman," he said, "poor bloody woman."

From the filling station where I sat dreaming in the sun, or from the enclosed office where I gazed mournfully at the rain, I would see, occasionally, Gleason entering or leaving his walled compound, a tiny figure way up on Bald Hill. And I'd think, "Gleason," but not much more.

Occasionally strangers drove up there to see what was going on, often egged on by locals who told them it was a Chinese temple or some other silly thing. Once a group of Italians had a picnic outside the walls and took photographs of each other standing in front of the closed door. God knows what they thought it was.

But for five years between my twelfth and seventeenth birthdays there was nothing to interest me in Gleason's walls. Those years seem lost to me now and I can remember very little of them. I developed a crush on Susy Markin and followed her back from the swimming pool on my bicycle. I sat behind her in the pictures and wandered past her house. Then her parents moved to another town and I sat in the sun and waited for them to come back.

We became very keen on modernization. When colored paints became available the whole town went berserk and brightly colored houses blossomed overnight. But the paints were not of good quality and quickly faded and peeled, so that the town looked like a garden of dead flowers. Thinking of those years, the only real thing I recall is the soft hiss of bicycle tires on the main street. When I think of it now it seems very peaceful, but I remember then that the sound induced in me a feeling of melancholy, a feeling somehow mixed with the early afternoons when the sun went down behind Bald Hill and the town felt as sad as an empty dance hall on a Sunday afternoon.

And then, during my seventeenth year, Mr. Gleason died. We found out when we saw Mrs. Gleason's pram parked out in front of Phonsey Joy's Funeral Parlor. It looked very sad, that pram, standing by itself in the windswept street. We came and looked at the pram and felt sad for Mrs. Gleason. She hadn't had much of a life.

Phonsey Joy carried old Mr. Gleason out to the cemetery by the Parwan Railway Station and Mrs. Gleason rode behind in a taxi. People watched the old hearse go by and thought, "Gleason," but not much else.

And then, less than a month after Gleason had been buried out at the lonely cemetery by the Parwan Railway Station, the Chinese laborers came back. We saw them push their bicycles up the hill. I stood with my father and Phonsey Joy and wondered what was going on.

And then I saw Mrs. Gleason trudging up the hill. I

nearly didn't recognize her, because she didn't have her pram. She carried a black umbrella and walked slowly up Bald Hill and it wasn't until she stopped for breath and leaned forward that I recognized her.

"It's Mrs. Gleason," I said, "with the Chinese."

But it wasn't until the next morning that it became obvious what was happening. People lined the main street in the way they do for a big funeral but, instead of gazing toward the Grant Street corner, they all looked up at Bald Hill.

All that day and all the next people gathered to watch the destruction of the walls. They saw the Chinese laborers darting to and fro, but it wasn't until they knocked down a large section of the wall facing the town that we realized there really was something inside. It was impossible to see what it was, but there was something there. People stood and wondered and pointed out Mrs. Gleason to each other as she went to and fro supervising the work.

And finally, in ones and twos, on bicycles and on foot, the whole town moved up to Bald Hill. Mr. Dyer closed up his butcher shop and my father got out the old Chevy truck and we finally arrived up at Bald Hill with twenty people on board. They crowded into the back tray and hung onto the running boards and my father grimly steered his way through the crowds of bicycles and parked just where the dirt track gets really steep. We trudged up this last steep track, never for a moment suspecting what we would find at the top.

It was very quiet up there. The Chinese laborers worked diligently, removing the third and fourth walls and cleaning the bricks, which they stacked neatly in big piles. Mrs. Gleason said nothing either. She stood in the only remain-

ing corner of the walls and looked defiantly at the townspeople, who stood openmouthed where another corner had
been.

And between us and Mrs. Gleason was the most incred-
ibly beautiful thing I had ever seen in my life. For one
moment I didn't recognize it. I stood openmouthed, and
breathed the surprising beauty of it. And then I realized it
was our town. The buildings were two feet high and they
were a little rough but very correct. I saw Mr. Dyer nudge
my father and whisper that Gleason had got the faded U in
the BUTCHER sign of his shop.

I think at that moment everyone was overcome with a
feeling of simple joy. I can't remember ever having felt so
uplifted and happy. It was perhaps a childish emotion, but
I looked up at my father and saw a smile of such warmth
spread across his face that I knew he felt just as I did. Later
he told me that he thought Gleason had built the model of
our town just for this moment, to let us see the beauty of
our own town, to make us proud of ourselves and to stop
the American dreams we were so prone to. For the rest, my
father said, was not Gleason's plan and he could not have
foreseen the things that happened afterward.

I have come to think that this view of my father's is a little sentimental and also, perhaps, insulting to Gleason. I
personally believe that he knew everything that would happen. One day the proof of my theory may be discovered.
Certainly there are in existence some personal papers, and
I firmly believe that these papers will show that Gleason
knew exactly what would happen.

We had been so overcome by the model of the town that

we hadn't noticed what was the most remarkable thing of all. Not only had Gleason built the houses and the shops of our town, he had also peopled it. As we tiptoed into the town we suddenly found ourselves. "Look," I said to Mr. Dyer, "there you are."

And there he was, standing in front of his shop in his apron. As I bent down to examine the tiny figure I was staggered by the look on its face. The modeling was crude, the paint work was sloppy, and the face a little too white, but the expression was absolutely perfect: those pursed, quizzical lips and the eyebrows lifted high. It was Mr. Dyer and no one else on earth.

And there beside Mr. Dyer was my father, squatting on the footpath and gazing lovingly at Mr. Dyer's bicycle's gears, his face marked with grease and hope.

And there was I, back at the filling station, leaning against a petrol pump in an American pose and talking to Brian Sparrow, who was amusing me with his clownish antics.

Phonsey Joy standing beside his hearse. Mr. Dixon sitting inside his hardware store. Everyone I knew was there in that tiny town. If they were not in the streets or in their backyards they were inside their houses, and it didn't take very long to discover that you could lift off the roofs and peer inside.

We tiptoed around the streets peeping into each other's windows, lifting off each other's roofs, admiring each other's gardens, and, while we did it, Mrs. Gleason slipped silently away down the hill toward Mason's Lane. She spoke to nobody and nobody spoke to her.

I confess that I was the one who took the roof from Cavanagh's house. So I was the one who found Mrs. Cavanagh in bed with young Craigie Evans.

I stood there for a long time, hardly knowing what I was seeing. I stared at the pair of them for a long, long time. And when I finally knew what I was seeing I felt such an incredible mixture of jealousy and guilt and wonder that I didn't know what to do with the roof.

Eventually it was Phonsey Joy who took the roof from my hands and placed it carefully back on the house, much, I imagine, as he would have placed the lid on a coffin. By then other people had seen what I had seen and the word passed around very quickly.

And then we all stood around in little groups and regarded the model town with what could only have been fear. If Gleason knew about Mrs. Cavanagh and Craigie Evans (and no one else had), what other things might he know? Those who hadn't seen themselves yet in the town began to look a little nervous and were unsure of whether to look for themselves or not. We gazed silently at the roofs and felt mistrustful and guilty.

We all walked down the hill then, very quietly, the way people walk away from a funeral, listening only to the crunch of the gravel under our feet while the women had trouble with their high-heeled shoes.

The next day a special meeting of the shire council passed a motion calling on Mrs. Gleason to destroy the model town on the grounds that it contravened building regulations.

It is unfortunate that this order wasn't carried out before

the city newspapers found out. Before another day had gone by the government had stepped in.

The model town and its model occupants were to be preserved. The minister for tourism came in a large black car and made a speech to us in the football pavilion. We sat on the high, tiered seats eating potato chips while he stood against the fence and talked to us. We couldn't hear him very well, but we heard enough. He called the model town a work of art and we stared at him grimly. He said it would be an invaluable tourist attraction. He said tourists would come from everywhere to see the model town. We would be famous. Our businesses would flourish. There would be work for guides and interpreters and caretakers and taxi drivers and people selling soft drinks and ice creams.

Americans would come, he said. They would visit our town in buses and in cars and on the train. They would take photographs and bring wallets bulging with dollars. American dollars.

We looked at the minister mistrustfully, wondering if he knew about Mrs. Cavanagh, and he must have seen the look because he said that certain controversial items would be removed, had already been removed. We shifted in our seats, like you do when a particularly tense part of a film has come to its climax, and then we relaxed and listened to what the minister had to say. And we all began, once more, to dream our American dreams.

We saw our big smooth cars cruising through cities with bright lights. We entered expensive nightclubs and danced till dawn. We made love to women like Kim Novak and men like Rock Hudson. We drank cocktails. We gazed lazily into refrigerators filled with food and prepared ourselves lavish midnight snacks that we ate while we watched huge television sets on which we would be able to see American movies free of charge and forever.

The minister, like someone from our American dreams, re-entered his large black car and cruised slowly from our humble sportsground, and the newspaper men arrived and swarmed over the pavilion with their cameras and note books. They took photographs of us and photographs of the models up on Bald Hill. And the next day we were all over the newspapers. The photographs of the model people side by side with photographs of the real people. And our names and ages and what we did were all printed there in black and white.

They interviewed Mrs. Gleason but she said nothing of interest. She said the model town had been her husband's hobby.

We all felt good now. It was very pleasant to have your photograph in the paper. And, once more, we changed our opinion of Gleason. The shire council held another meeting and named the dirt track up Bald Hill, "Gleason Avenue." Then we all went home and waited for the Americans we had been promised.

It didn't take long for them to come, although at the time it seemed an eternity, and we spent six long months doing nothing more with our lives than waiting for the Americans.

Well, they did come. And let me tell you how it has all worked out for us.

The Americans arrive every day in buses and cars and sometimes the younger ones come on the train. There is now a small airstrip out near the Parwan cemetery and they also arrive there, in small airplanes. Phonsey Joy drives them to the cemetery where they look at Gleason's grave and then up to Bald Hill and then down to the town. He is doing very well from it all. It is good to see someone doing well from it. Phonsey is becoming a big man in town and is on the shire council.

On Bald Hill there are half a dozen telescopes through which the Americans can spy on the town and reassure themselves that it is the same down there as it is on Bald Hill. Herb Gravney sells them ice creams and soft drinks and extra film for their cameras. He is another one who is doing well. He bought the whole model from Mrs. Gleason and charges five American dollars admission. Herb is on the council now too. He's doing very well for himself. He sells them the film so they can take photographs of the houses and the model people and so they can come down to the town with their special maps and hunt out the real people.

To tell the truth most of us are pretty sick of the game. They come looking for my father and ask him to stare at the gears of Dyer's bicycle. I watch my father cross the street slowly, his head hung low. He doesn't greet the Americans anymore. He doesn't ask them questions about color television or Washington, D.C. He kneels on the footpath in front of Dyer's bike. They stand around him. Often they remember the model incorrectly and try to get my father to pose in the wrong way. Originally he argued with them, but now he argues no more. He does what they ask. They push him this way and that and worry about the expression on his face which is no longer what it was.

Then I know they will come to find me. I am next on the map. I am very popular for some reason. They come in search of me and my petrol pump as they have done for four years now. I do not await them eagerly because I know, before they reach me, that they will be disappointed.

"But this is not the boy."

"Yes," says Phonsey, "this is him alright." And he gets me to show them my certificate.

They examine the certificate suspiciously, feeling the paper as if it might be a clever forgery. "No," they declare. (Americans are so confident.) "No," they shake their heads, "this is not the real boy. The real boy is younger."

"He's older now. He used to be younger." Phonsey looks weary when he tells them. He can afford to look weary.

The Americans peer at my face closely. "It's a different boy."

But finally they get their cameras out. I stand sullenly and try to look amused as I did once. Gleason saw me looking amused but I can no longer remember how it felt. I was looking at Brian Sparrow. But Brian is also tired. He finds it difficult to do his clownish antics and to the Americans his little act isn't funny. They prefer the model. I watch him sadly, sorry that he must perform for such an unsympathetic audience.

The Americans pay one dollar for the right to take our photographs. Having paid the money they are worried about being cheated. They spend their time being disappointed and I spend my time feeling guilty, that I have somehow let them down by growing older and sadder.

Glossary

bagman: tramp

bally, balley: euphemism for the vulgar expression "bloody."

billy, billy can: a tin or enamelware container with a close-fitting lid, used for making tea or cooking over open fire.

biro: ballpoint pen.

boot: car trunk.

bounce: kickoff in an Australian Rules football game.

boundary rider: one who rides around the boundaries of a station (ranch) mending fences, etc.

brumby: wild or unbroken horse.

Bundy: abbreviation for Bundenburg rum.

Centennial Park: a major park in Sydney; opened in 1888 to celebrate 100 years of European settlement.

Cherry Ripe: favorite Australian chocolate bar.

choko: succulent cucumber-like vegetable.

coach: bus.

cockies: derogatory term for dairy farmers.

Cockney dudes: pretentious politicians with questionable backgrounds.

crook: dishonest, unscrupulous.

curlew: long-billed wading bird with musical cry.

dilly bag: small bag or basket.

doss: to sleep.

Dreamtime, Dreaming; also **Alchera, Alcheringa:** the golden age in Aboriginal mythology when the world and the first ancestors were created.

Dry: season of drought.

Façade: English ballet based on Edith Sitwell's poetry.

fibro: fiber board used for house construction.

flog: sell.

galah: rose-breasted, gray-backed cockatoo.

gin: derogatory term for female Aborigine.

gnamma hole: natural waterhole.

Governor: reference to Captain Arthur Phillip (1738–1814) who led the First Fleet to Australia in 1788 and served as the colony's first governor.

hessian: strong, coarse cloth of mixed hemp and jute.

HSC: Higher School Certificate that permits entrance to a university.

humpy: hut or shanty.

Hurd Hatfield: the actor who portrayed Dorian Gray in the 1945 film, *The Picture of Dorian Gray*.

lift: elevator.

mallee: scrub formed by eucalypts in arid areas.

metho: methylated spirits; a person who drinks metho.

mulga: shrubby acacia that grows densely in parts of Australia.

mullock: rock.

Myers: Sydney department store.

nongaru: initiation ground for Aboriginal women.

Nullarbor Plain: vast desert separating eastern and western Australia.

paddock: fenced piece of land.

pannikin: small, metal drinking utensil.

Parramatta: a working-class suburb of Sydney.

pash off: passionate embrace; literally "passion off."

plum-duff: doughy plum pudding.

saloon: station wagon; panel truck.

serviette: napkin.

shout; shout the bar: to treat someone; to order drinks for everyone.

Kenneth Slessor: highly-regarded modernist poet from Sydney (1901–71).

Arthur Streeton: popular Australian painter who captured the country's distinctive landscape (1867–1943).

swagman: tramp.

swingle-tree: pivoted bar to which traces are attached on a plough.

take-away: takeout food.

Tobaccotown, Mango, Reeftown: Thea Astley's names for Northern Queensland towns.

track: rough, poorly constructed road; marks left by passage.

tucker: food.

ute: utility vehicle

WA: Western Australia.

White House: jocular reference to the Sydney home of Patrick White, the reclusive and eccentric writer who was Australia's only Nobel Laureate in literature.

Wongi: name of an Aboriginal tribe.

willy-willy: whirlwind.

Contributors

ROBERT ROSS is a Research Associate at the Edward A. Clark Center for Australian Studies, University of Texas at Austin, where he edits *Antipodes—A North American Journal of Australian Literature and Culture*, now in its twelfth year of publication. In addition to publishing numerous articles on the new literatures in English, he is the author of *Australian Literary Criticism— 1945–1988* and editor of *International Literature in English—Essays on the Major Writers*. His study of an Australian novelist, *Parables of Displacement—Thea Astley's Fiction*, will be published by the University of Queensland Press.

~

THEA ASTLEY (1925–) was born in Brisbane, the capital of the tropical state of Queensland, which serves as the setting for most of her fiction. She has published two short story collections and fourteen novels, the first in 1958, the most recent, *The Multiple Effects of Rainshadow*, in 1996. Having taught in public schools and later in the university for most of her life, Astley is now retired and continues to write. She has received many awards and prizes for her work, including the Patrick White Prize and the Prime Minister's Arts Fellowship. With the American publication of *Beachmasters* in 1985 and the reissue of her earlier novels, Astley has gained recognition overseas.

MURRAY BAIL (1941–) records the absurdity he sees dominating modern life. Publishing short stories for the most part, Bail moves between the experimental and the conventional in technique. This approach also prevails in his novel, *Homesickness*, which satirizes Australians abroad on a package tour. "The Life of the Party," Bail's wry look at suburbia, comes from *The Drover's Wife and Other Stories*, the main story being an irreverent, updated version of Henry Lawson's classic tale with the same title. Bail, born in Adelaide, lived abroad for several years before settling in Sydney.

BARBARA BAYNTON (1857–1929) started her life humbly in a New South Wales country town but after several marriages—one gaining her the title of "Lady"—she established herself as an international society figure moving between England and Australia. Although she did not publish extensively, her short novel, *Human Toll*, and collection of short stories, *Bush Studies*, from which "The Chosen Vessel" is taken, have gained her a place in Australian literature. Feminist critics, in particular, admire Baynton's determined portrayal of female characters caught up in what she called the "awful waste" of the Australian bush.

PETER CAREY (1943–) received the Booker Prize in 1988 for his novel about colonial Australia, *Oscar & Lucinda*. His first book of short stories, *The Fat Man in History*, which contains "American Dreams," appeared in 1974. Since then he has published another short story collection, six novels, and a children's book. Born in a country town in Victoria, Carey was educated in Australia, lived in London briefly, then returned to Sydney, where he worked in an advertising agency. Now writing full time, Carey lives in New York. "American Dreams" illustrates the original form and range of Carey's work, which moves from the debunking of Australian history in *Illywhacker* to the creation of an imaginary post-colonial nation in *The Unusual Life of Tristan Smith*.

ELEANOR DARK (1901–1985) is best known for her trilogy that traces the British settlement of Australia from 1788 to 1814 and explores the conflict between European and Aboriginal world views. The selection called "The First Gathering" comes from *The Timeless Land*, which was followed by *Storm of Time* and *No Barrier*. This excerpt describing the First Fleet of convicts and their keepers, along with the Aboriginal observers, typifies the subtle way Dark handles historical material and actual personages throughout the trilogy. Born in Sydney, Dark lived most of her life in the Blue Mountains west of the city.

ROBERT DREWE (1943–), born in Melbourne, was educated in Western Australia and started his journalistic career there. His first novel, *The Savage Crows*, tracks the destruction of the Tasmanian Aborigines through the portrayal of a contemporary researcher who becomes obsessed with the tragic events of the nineteenth century. Set in part on Sydney's famed Bondi Beach, "Stingray" comes from *The Body Surfers*, a short story collection that scrutinizes Australian beach culture and city life.

HELEN GARNER (1942–) was born in Geelong, near Melbourne, and graduated from the University of Melbourne. She taught for several years in Melbourne secondary schools until she was dismissed for answering students' questions about sex. This disruption of her teaching career led her into journalism, then into fiction writing. Garner's novels such as *Monkey Grip* and *The Children's Bach* speak for the young, educated, urban Australian —the literary territory she has defined and refined. After living in Paris for several years and serving as a visiting professor at New York University, Garner now lives in Sydney. She continues to write both fiction and nonfiction, and currently contributes columns on film to *The Australian's Review of Books*. "Postcards from Surfers" comes from Garner's collection of short stories with the same title.

XAVIER HERBERT (1901–1984), a native of Western Australia, continued to write in the bush tradition long after it became unfashionable. He used its conventions to indict his fellow Australians' behavior, in particular their treatment of Aborigines and their disregard for the environment. The literary spokesman for the Northern Territory and its major town of Darwin, Herbert represents the outback and its inhabitants forcefully in his two best-known novels, *Capricornia*—his name for the Territory, and the sprawling and lengthy *Poor Fellow My Country*. Published in its present form for the first time in 1990, "Misanthropy" is a revision of one of Herbert's early stories.

JANETTE TURNER HOSPITAL (1942–) grew up in Australia and since 1971 has lived in Canada. Her first novel, *The Ivory Swing*, appeared in 1982 to critical acclaim. In the years following she has published steadily, gained an international reputation, and received numerous awards for a fiction that often focuses on personal displacement. She was named one of Canada's "Ten Best Young Fiction Writers." Although Hospital does not always set her work in Australia, "You Gave Me Hyacinths" draws from her experience as a teacher in Northern Queensland.

ELIZABETH JOLLEY (1923–) emigrated from England to Perth, Western Australia, in 1959. Born in Birmingham, she was educated in England and Europe, and worked as a nurse during World War II. She wrote fiction for many years before her sudden emergence as a significant writer in 1976 when *Five Acre Virgin and Other Stories* appeared. Since then she has received international attention for her novels, such as *Mr. Scobie's Riddle* and *Foxybaby*, as well as for other collections of short stories, including *Woman in a Lampshade*, from which "Pear Tree Dance" comes. Jolley's wry, sometimes gothic, always compassionate fiction focuses on the dreams and trials, failures and minor triumphs of ordinary people. Her work is drawn in part from her

British background and in part from her adopted country. Jolley lives in Perth, where she continues to write and to contribute to Western Australia's thriving literary life as a creative writing teacher.

C.J. KOCH (1932–) is widely known for *The Year of Living Dangerously*, set in Indonesia during the upheaval before Sukarno's fall. Born in the island state of Tasmania, Koch recalls his boyhood there in his first novel, *The Boys in the Island*; in his recent book *Highways to a War* he opens with a Tasmanian setting before moving the action to Asia. "Return to Hobart Town" appears in Koch's book of memoirs and essays, *Crossing the Gap*.

HENRY LAWSON (1867–1922), who could be called Australia's Mark Twain, was born in New South Wales and grew up in the bush. As a young man he moved to Sydney, where he held odd jobs while establishing himself as a journalist, then as a poet of bush life and social protest, finally as a short story writer, which was his true calling. Most of his realistic—sometimes comic, sometimes tragic—portrayals of bush life stem from his childhood and later experiences in the outback, even though he spent most of his life in Sydney.

DAVID MALOUF (1934–) has gained wide recognition for his fiction. In 1996 he was the first recipient of the International IMPAC Dublin Literary Award for the metaphorical novel about Australia's settlement, *Remembering Babylon*. Born in Brisbane of Syrian descent, Malouf has set much of his work in that city, but he has also written about World War II in *The Great World* and ancient times in *An Imaginary Life*. The classic themes of bushranging and the convict experience take on allegorical meaning in Malouf's 1996 novel *The Conversations at Curlow Creek*. "A Medium" appeared in *Antipodes*, a short story collection.

OODGEROO NOONUCCAL (1920–1993) originally published as Kath Walker but in 1988 took her tribal name. Born in Brisbane,

Oodgeroo pioneered Aboriginal writing in English when she published her first volume of poetry, *We Are Going*, in 1964. She remained active in Aboriginal cultural affairs throughout her life, and received numerous awards for the work she carried out.

KABUL OODGEROO NOONUCCAL (1953–) is Oodgeroo's son. Trained both in theater and painting, he continues to work in performing and visual arts in Australia and abroad.

KATHARINE SUSANNAH PRICHARD (1883–1969) devoted her energy to politics and writing, which some critics have noted were not always compatible. A founding member of the Communist Party of Australia, Prichard is at her best when she writes about a nonpolitical Western Australia, where she spent most of her life. "The Old Track" appears in *Tribute, Selected Stories*, a recent collection of Prichard's work.

STEELE RUDD (1868–1935), the pseudonym for Arthur Hoey Davis, based his farcical accounts of bush life on his own family's experiences, even though the "Rudd" family members were not actually drawn from real life. Born in the Queensland bush, he was a prolific writer and immensely popular in his day. He followed a formulaic pattern that recounted the misadventures of families working "selections"—pieces of land granted free by the government. "We Embark in the Bear Industry" is a chapter from *Stocking Our Selection*.

MANDY SAYER (1963–) published her first novel in 1988. Since then two more novels have appeared. Sayer was born and grew up in Sydney near King's Cross, which figures in her 1995 novel about urban renewal, *The Cross*, and in the short story that appears in this anthology. An accomplished tap dancer, she has performed and taught dance. Sayer, who holds degrees in creative writing from Indiana University, currently lives in King's Cross and is working on a Ph.D. in English at the University of Sydney.

ARTHUR UPFIELD (1892–1964) came to Australia from England when he was eighteen. Intrigued by the outback, he led a nomadic life in the bush where he worked at odd jobs and gathered material for his detective novels—rich with bush lore, Aboriginal customs, landscape, and mateship. Each book features the part-Aboriginal detective-inspector "Bony," who has gained admirers the world over. Taken from *The Sands of Windee*, "At the Source of Life" depicts the tension between the demands of civilization and the fragility of the land, a recurrent Upfield theme.

JUDAH WATEN (1911–1985) emigrated with his family from Russia in 1914, settling first in Western Australia, then in Melbourne where he remained until his death. The author of seven novels as well as memoirs, essays, and short stories, Waten based some of his work on his immigrant family's adjustment to the new country—a theme that "Mother" forcefully carries out. It appeared originally in *Alien Son*, a collection of stories inspired by Waten's childhood.

ARCHIE WELLER (1957–) is a poet and fiction writer who was born in Western Australia and grew up in Perth. Although his Aboriginal heritage has been disputed recently, he insists that his sensibility is Aboriginal. And his writing carries out that claim with its sympathetic concern over the plight of the urban Aborigine. His first novel, *The Day of the Dog*, appeared in 1982, and his book of short stories, *Going Home*, which includes "Pension Day," was published in 1986.

PATRICK WHITE (1912–1990) received the Nobel Prize for Literature in 1973. The author of twelve novels, three collections of short fiction, and eight plays, White showed a tremendous range, both stylistically and thematically. Born into a wealthy landowning Australian family, he graduated from Cambridge, served in World War II, and returned to Sydney in 1945, where he lived until his death. "The O'Dowds at Home," as it is titled in this collection, is chapter 10 from *The Tree of Man*, a novel that White described as an attempt to discover the "extraordinary" in the "ordinary"—an apt description for all of his impressive body of work.

MICHAEL WILDING (1942–) was born in England and emigrated to Australia in the 1960s. Since then he has taught in the English Department at the University of Sydney. A witty, cosmopolitan, experimental writer, Wilding has through his short stories refined and redefined the urban experience. Much of his fiction examines writers themselves and the process of storytelling. He has also gained a reputation as an astute literary critic and scholar.

TIM WINTON (1960–) published his first novel, *An Open Swimmer*, when he was twenty-two, and has since established himself as one of Australia's major writers. His 1991 novel *Cloudstreet* received international attention for its imaginative account of two families in Perth. Winton was born in Western Australia, where he still lives. It is from this remote area and its people that he draws his material, which he transforms into a compassionate and often humorous examination of contemporary life.

B. WONGAR (1936–) is the pseudonym for Sreten Bozíc, a Serbian immigrant to Australia. When he arrived in the late 1950s he lived in the Northern Territory with Aborigines. From them he learned tribal social structures, customs, and mythology, as well as their respect for the sanctity of the land. Since 1970 B. Wongar has published numerous short stories based on Aboriginal mythology, especially that connected with the dingo, such as "Dingo's Picnic." "The Nuclear Trilogy" (*Walg, Karan,* and *Gabo Djara*) describes the effects of nuclear testing on Aborigines and the environment. In his recent novel, *Raki*, he combines Serbian history with the Aboriginal experience. B. Wongar lives in Melbourne with several dingoes.

Permissions

Eleanor Dark's "The First Gathering" is excerpted from *The Timeless Land*, published by Fontana Books, © 1941, 1973. Reprinted by permission of Curtis Brown (Aust) Pty Ltd.

B. Wongar's "Dingo's Picnic" was originally published in *Antipodes*. © 1987 B. Wongar, reprinted by permission of the author.

Arthur Upfield's "At the Source of Life" is from *The sands of Windee*, published by Scribner and Sons, © 1931 Arthur Upfield

Barbara Baynton's "The Chosen Vessel" was reprinted by permission of University of Queensland Press.

Steel Rudd's "We Embark in the Bear Industry" was reprinted by permission of University of Queensland Press.

Xavier Herbert's "Misanthropy" from *South of Capricon*, published by University of Oxford Press, © 1990 Robyn Sinclair. Reprinted by permission of copyright owner and Curtis Brown (Aust) Pty Ltd. This is a revised version of "Philanthropy," originally published in 1933.

Patrick White's "The O'Dowds at Home" from *The Tree of Life* was published by Penguin Books Australia, © 1955 Patrick White. Reprinted by permission of The Barbara Mobbs Agency.

Elizabeth Jolley's "Pear Tree Dance" from *Woman in a Lampshade* was published by Penguin Australia, © 1983 Elizabeth Jolley. Reprinted by permission of Penguin Australia.

Janette Turner Hospital's "You Gave Me Hyacinths" from *Dislocations* was published by University of Queensland Press, © 1986 Janette Turner Hospital. Reprinted by permission of the author, University of Queensland Press, and Louisiana State University Press.

Tim Winton's "Thomas Awkner Floats" from *Scission,* published by McPhee Gribble, Australia, © 1985 Tim Winton. Reprinted by permis-